TEARDROPS

and

tiny trailers

DOUGLAS KEISTER

TEARDROPS
and
tiny trailers

Gibbs Smith, Publisher
TO ENRICH AND INSPIRE HUMANKIND
Salt Lake City | Charleston | Santa Fe | Santa Barbara

TO JOHN LOUDON MCADAM (1756-1836)

FIRST EDITION
16 15 14 13 12   7 8 9 10

PUBLISHED BY
Gibbs Smith, Publisher
P.O. Box 667
Layton, Utah 84041

Orders: 1.800.835.4993
www.gibbs-smith.com

Designed by Michel Vrána, blackeye.com
Gibbs Smith books are printed on paper produced from sustainable PEFC-certified forest/controlled wood source. Learn more at: www.pefc.org
Printed and bound in Hong Kong

Library of Congress Cataloging-in-Publication Data

Keister, Douglas.
  Teardrops and tiny trailers / Douglas Keister. – 1st ed.
    p. cm.
  ISBN-13: 978-1-4236-0274-3
  ISBN-10: 1-4236-0274-9
  1. Travel trailers—History. 2. Travel trailers—Pictorial works. 3. Antique and classic cars—Collectors and collecting. I. Title.

TL297.K3825 2008
629.226–dc22
                    2008000723

Contents

Acknowledgments

Thanks to all the trailerites who gave their time and trailers to make *Teardrops and Tiny Trailers* a beautiful book: Ray Allen, Bob Ambrose, Don and DeAnna Anderson, Ed Avila, Tom and Mary Bamborough, Jean and Jeanne Bayol, Steve and Peggy Birley, Forrest and Jeri Bone, Terry and Michelle Bone, Joe Bosier, John Bosier, Paul Broxon, Wendy Case, Linda and Don Coolich, Doug Cronn, Michelle and Ken Defer, Henry and Janell Diaz, Timothy Dillon, Jim Eddy, Gordie and Terry Engelstad, Bill Eosel, Patrick and Joanne Ewing, Ken and Petey Faber, Wayne Fergusson, Tammy Fuller, Mark and Rhonda Gelstein, Rod Glassett, John Green, Larry Grim, Jerome Guffey, Gerry and Rod Hagelund, James Hamilton, Charlie Hanson, Doug Hardekopf, Phil and Esther Harmon, Chris Hart, Michael and Aedan Haworth, Dan Hazard, Al Hesselbart, Luke Hinman, Douglas Hoder, Craig and Patti Holroyd, Stuart and Kathleen Honnard, Wendy and Steven Hughes-Jelen, Mardy Ireland, Debbie Izenman, Bob Johnson, Barbara and Donald Jussero, Steven Katkowsky, Ed and Linda Kelson, Leo and Marlys Keoshian, James Larimore, Gary and Sally Lodholm, Steve and Candy Marino, Norm and Ann Markus, Jerry and Jenean Marlette, Vince Martinico, Ken and Marty Masden, Dave Mikol, Bob and Cindy Mott, Rick and Janice Myer, David Nathenson, Shannon and Cecily Near, James Nelson, Lori Osborne, Charles Panter, Gail Parker, Cliff Parker, Ken Patten, Steve Pepper, Lew and Lesley Puls, Robin and Kevin Ramos, Steve Robison, Damian and Sandra Rutherford, Phil Schaeffer, Sandy Smelser, Mike and Debbie Smith, Emil and Ed Sokolis, Louise Stein, Cullen Tate, Charles Taylor, Dayton Taylor, Dean Tennis, Keith and Barb Thompson, Rando and Lori Thyr, Lowell and Janice Vivian, Rich and Mary Vock, Duke and Fay Waldrop, Tammy and Steven Walker, Bill Walter, Ross Westerbur, Grant Whipp, Gar and Mary Alice Williams

Special thanks go to Gibbs Smith, Publisher, for believing in my vision, to my agent Julie Castiglia for shepherding the book through, and, as always, to my wife Sandra Mclean, my self-proclaimed biggest fan.

THE ROAD

A h, the Road! That shimmering, steaming ribbon of asphalt that criss-crosses the country. It's the stuff of adventure—the promise of new horizons, new people, a new life. Because we tend to group together, sometimes we just need to break away. No longer passive cows, we make a mad dash for greener pastures and bigger and bluer skies. In earlier times, Gulliver traveled and Twain roughed it. Germans call it wanderlust, Aussies take off on a walkabout, and Brits go on a bimble.

The road is the great democratizer, available to anyone with a set of wheels and a few coins of the realm. Whether our transporters are mopeds or Maseratis, the sinuous black macadam is available to all. The road trip is fodder for great novels. Steinbeck traveled with an aged poodle named Charley. William Least Heat Moon stayed in the slow lane along America's blue highways. And Jack Kerouac went on the road for the quintessential voyage of self-discovery. Taking a road trip is a rite of passage for many, a way to collect one's thoughts during times of transition: youth to adulthood, classrooms to the working world, single life to marriage, marriage to singlehood.

Despite our romantic visions of the road, for most folks the road is merely an expedient way to get from point A to point B. We rely on the electronic brains of the Internet and satellite-driven GPS devices to guide us to our destination. The quicker and straighter, the better. But there is one group of humans who thinks they have a better way. These latter-day Argonauts are recreational vehicle enthusiasts, better known as RVers. Many are retired or semiretired and are in no particular hurry to get to their destination, if they even have one. They don't need to get to their reserved hotel or motel room. Like the turtle and hermit crab, they take their shelter wherever they go.

Because of their Brobdingnagian proportions, we tend to notice the mega-motorhomes more than any other type. In spite of rising fuel prices, there seem to be more and more of these rolling homes every year. Interestingly and almost concurrent with the swelling number and girth of RVs, there has been a trend toward compact motorhomes and trailers. As these proportion-conscious consumers search for smaller transporters, they are also rediscovering older RVs, often tucked away in garages, barns, and sheds, or moldering away in backyards and pastures. This rediscovery of vintage RVs began in the 1980s when fans of the sleek and silvery Airstream trailers formed a club that was an offshoot of the Airstream Club. Appropriately dubbed the Vintage Airstream Club, its membership steadily grew throughout the 1980s and '90s, so much so that fans of vintage Airstreams soon began to find other vintage trailers and motorhomes. Owners of these non-Airstreams couldn't register their trailers with the Vintage Airstream Club, so two members, Forrest and Jeri Bone, resurrected an ancient RVer's organization called the Tin Can Tourists (established in 1919) and opened it to owners of all brands of vintage RVs. Tin Can Tourists rallies now attract well over one hundred vintage trailers and motorhomes.

One of the most interesting types of vintage trailers that were being extracted from their moorings are little trailers known as teardrops. These marvels of compact camping have a sleeping area about the size of a piece of plywood and an aft exterior kitchen. The first proponents of these newly resurrected trailers were the vintage car enthusiasts who liked the way the sensuous form of their classic automobiles worked together with the trailer. There has been such a demand for these tidy rolling bedrooms that a number of companies have started manufacturing complete trailers or supplying kits and plans. Other enthusiasts have been restoring "canned ham" trailers, so called because their ovoid shape resembles a can of ham. Then there are the Airstream aficionados. These silver gems and their cousins made by other companies are perhaps the most easily identifiable vintage trailers, thanks to their distinctive shape and glistening finish.

Whether traveling in a tiny teardrop trailer or a diesel-belching lumbering leviathan, RVers have discovered that there is much to be said for living life in the slow lane. Buckle up and enjoy the visual feast in the pages that follow. You'll find that bigger is not always better, and being able to take along a tidy little home on wheels opens up a whole new way of seeing the country.

BY THE MID-1950S, thanks largely to America's postwar prosperity and an aggressive road building plan by the Eisenhower administration, trailers had attained enormous proportions. The June 1955 issue of *Science and Mechanics* magazine depicts a 16-foot canned-ham-style trailer dwarfed by a 40-foot house trailer.

THE BIBLE for do-it-yourself trailer builders in the late 1930s was this paperback tome published in 1937 by Modern Mechanix Publishing Company. The company also published the monthly magazine *Modern Mechanix*. The book's 132 pages are packed with plans for a variety of travel and utility trailers plus automotive tips such as how to convert a steering wheel into a writing desk, how to turn a starter motor into a polisher, and how to make a wind generator that mounts to the top of your car.

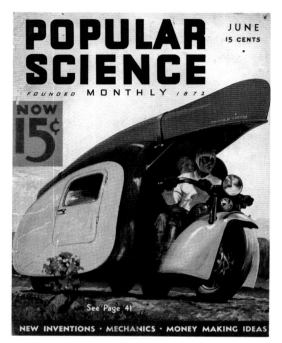

AN UNNAMED GERMAN INVENTOR is credited with the design of this teardrop trailer towed by a motorcycle that appeared on the cover of the June 1936 issue of *Popular Science* magazine. A short article included basic plans and drawings, but it's unclear if any units were ever constructed.

THE YEARS immediately after World War II were the heyday of teardrops and tiny trailers. Every popular handyman magazine was chockfull of plans and advertisements for diminutive trailers. The February 1951 issue of *Popular Homecraft* included detailed plans for the 8-foot-long Wander Pup trailer that could be built from eight sheets of plywood and 1 x 2-inch pine strips on a prefabricated steel frame. The Wander Pup weighed in at 700 pounds and could easily be towed by any vehicle.

DER KLEIN PRINZ, the smallest Airstream ever made , hits the road at Camp Dearborn, Michigan. For more information on this trailer, see the chapter entitled Silver Gems.

IN AN ERA of large, jumbo, and super-sized proportioned RVs, this stylish combo illustrates that you can have a tow vehicle, trailer, and boat all in the same compact package. This 1956 Cadillac Sedan DeVille has enough power to tow a 1956 Kom-Pak trailer down the road like a sack of feathers.

TEARDROP FANS point to this article published in the September 1947 issue of *Mechanix Illustrated* magazine as the article that launched the teardrop craze. Throughout the late 1940s and early 1950s, handymen and small manufacturers produced these gems in their garages and small shops. Teardrop trailers saw a second coming in the 1990s fueled by vintage car enthusiasts and vintage trailer clubs.

Above: Standard hitch connects trailer and car. Threaded caster levels body floor when parked.

BUILD WITH BLUEPRINTS
Mechanix Illustrated conducts a blueprint and plan service for its readers. You will find a partial list of available blueprints and plans on page 162.

TRAILER for TWO

A streamlined home on wheels that's light and easily towed; has a double-berth and complete kitchenette.

"GETTING away from it all" doesn't mean giving up the comforts of home, for with this compact camp trailer you bring them right along with you. As it's only a fraction of the size and weight of a full-grown trailer, you can take this 10-ft. tourer wherever a car will go. And when you reach some ideal spot beside a lake or stream, up goes the hood over the kitchenette and in a matter of minutes there's an appetizing meal cooking away on the pull-out stove. Under the same hood, there's an icebox (for the big ones that didn't get away), a water tank, folding table and cupboard space for a raft of food.

a full-length mattress waiting for you when you turn in. And if you like fresh air when you sleep, just open the screened-in panels on the doors.

Original trailer designed by Howard Warren of Riverside, Calif. has travelled thousands of miles

ting headroom... storage space for clothes... electric light for reading in bed.

Now let's take a look at the drawings on these pages and then get on with the actual construction. The trailer has a welded angle-iron chassis that's illustrated in Fig. 2 This doesn't extend the full length of the body so that you can remove the camp body and substitute an open box type. If this might give your wife ideas about building a rock garden, then make the chassis the full length of the body and play safe.

The chassis should be built up of ¼ by 2 by 2 in. angle iron, mitered and welded at

TEARDROP
Trailers

IT HAS OFTEN BEEN SAID THAT OWNERS OF TRAVEL TRAILERS

(and especially vintage travel trailers) are some of the friendliest people on earth.

Sociologists tell us that we humans are herd animals and tend to group together.

When we live in our bolted-down homes, we are a bit reluctant to befriend other

members of the herd (our neighbors) until we've gotten to know them a bit. Not

so with RVers. They are a naturally gregarious lot for the simple reason that if

things don't work out with their neighbors, they can easily move.

t also appears to be true that the smaller the RV, the friendlier the owner. We've all heard stories of folks who pull up to a campground in their enormous bus-like motorhome. One of the occupants scampers out, attaches the necessary utility hookups, and steals back inside. The next thing we see is the flickering azure glow of a jumbo plasma screen, followed by the intoxicating aroma of microwave popcorn. Early the next morning the mysterious RV pulls out of the campground in a fog of diesel smoke and rumbles on down the road. However, right next to the lumbering motorhome may be a teardrop trailer. Its owners have set up a small awning, pulled out a couple of lawn chairs, and are happily greeting their fellow campers. Despite the Lilliputian size of the trailer, everyone wants a look at the inside. Its owners are more than happy to oblige. The fact of the matter is, the teardrop's owners are forced to be more social since spending more time in their tiny abode than it takes to sleep is a bit claustrophobic.

There has been an enormous increase in the popularity of teardrop trailers in recent years. Most people think these trailers emerged after World War II, but they have a long, rich history dating back to the Great Depression. Since most of the early teardrops were homebuilt, it's hard to plumb the exact date of the first true teardrop trailer. A strong candidate for the first formally manufactured teardrop trailer with an aft exterior kitchen is the Kaycraft Kampster, plans for which appeared in the December 1936 issue of *Outdoor Life* magazine. The trailer, which used a 4 x 10-foot sheet of plywood secured to a steel frame, was designed by Walter Hille and J. S. McBeth of Los Angeles. *Outdoor Life* published a detailed two-part article and also offered "a complete set of two blueprints" for fifty cents. Interestingly, a similar-shaped trailer without a rear kitchen appeared in the December 1936 issue of *Mechanics and Handicraft* magazine. That magazine has one of the earliest references to the name "teardrop" when describing a crawl-in trailer with the distinctive teardrop shape. There is also anecdotal information that some home-built teardrop trailers may have been made as early as 1933 or 1934. Throughout the late 1930s, handyman-oriented magazines were chock-full of a variety of plans for these tidy little trailers. Eventually companies started manufacturing ready-to-assemble kits and complete trailers.

Understandably, World War II put the brakes on most types of trailers, but after the war, companies that sold plans, kits, and fully assembled teardrops were back in full force. Many teardrop fans point to the September 1947 issue of *Mechanix Illustrated* magazine as the genesis of the postwar teardrop revival. That magazine had a six-page article titled "A Trailer For Two."

There were mom-and-pop trailer manufacturers, which manufactured a few trailers, as well as more formal factories. Most of the manufacturers were in the Los Angeles area and catered to the outdoor-oriented lifestyle of the region. Among the most popular teardrop trailers were the following:

KIT

The most enduring of all the teardrop brands is the Kit Kamper. The company was started immediately after World War II in October 1945 by C. W. "Bill" Worman and Andy Anderson. Their company, which they headquartered in the shell of an abandoned fruit stand in Norwalk, California, was christened the Kit Manufacturing Company. The duo planned to offer the trailer as a kit (hence the name) but had few orders. A short time later a friend of Worman's, Dan Pocapalia, bought out Anderson's share for $800. After analyzing the less-than-stellar sales, Worman and Pocapalia decided to offer the Kit Kamper fully assembled rather than as a kit. The first 4 x 8-foot units were offered to dealers at a trade show in February 1946 for $500. The enthusiastic dealers placed orders for over 500 trailers, which prompted Worman and Pocapalia to design and offer an upgraded model with additional cosmetic features for $595. The factory-made units can be identified with the V-shaped graphic on the back cover. By July 1946, the

company had backorders for over one thousand trailers. By the end of 1947, over 4,500 Kit Kampers had rolled out the door. Interestingly, the company decided to abandon the teardrop line in 1948 and concentrate on more conventional travel trailers. Eventually the company became a manufacturer of higher-end RVs and manufactured housing.

KEN-SKILL

Ken-Skill teardrops are among some of the most desirable vintage teardrops because of their timeless design, which makes them easy to pair up with almost any tow vehicle. They were manufactured in Burbank, California, in the late 1940s.

MODERNISTIC, CUB, MODERNAIRE, AND MARVEL DWYER TEARDROP TRAILERS

These shiny aluminum trailers were made in the late 1940s by Prefabricated Trailer Manufacturing and Modernistic Trailer Manufacturing located in the Los Angeles area. They were distributed by National Trailer Stores, also based in Los Angeles. Ads for the Modernistic, which were available as kits for $280 or fully assembled for $500, appeared regularly in popular handyman magazines throughout the 1940s.

BENROY

Despite its 4 x 8-foot footprint, the Benroy trailer is roomier than most teardrops because of its stubbier profile, which sacrifices some of the streamlined teardrop shape but allows for an increased cargo area and a more accessible kitchen. The Benroy name was adapted from the firm's founders, designer Bennet Petersen and investor Roy Greenwood. The company churned out about 480 units, which sold for $420, from its Burbank, California, factory from 1953 to 1955. The Benroy's galley was equipped with a two-burner propane stove, porcelain sink, twenty-five-pound icebox, and six-gallon water tank. A trailer dealership, King Richard's of El Monte, California, acquired the Benroy's molds after Benroy went out of business and produced a few trailers under the King Richard brand.

SCAD-A-BOUT

The Scad-A-Bout teardrop, manufactured in

Pasadena, California, has a profile very much like the Benroy, but the rear hatch of the trailer looks more like a standard automobile trunk and does not go all the way to the ground.

TOURETTE

The Tourette (also known as Tourer) was manufactured by the Universal Trailer Corporation of Kansas City, Missouri, from the early to mid-1940s to the early 1950s. They weighed about 720 pounds and came with a luggage rack, icebox, and stove. They sold for about $750 in 1947.

KAMP MASTER, CAMPMASTER, WILD GOOSE

These jumbo teardrops are best described as a teardrop on steroids. They have an oversize hatch that opens far enough to allow egress into the entire rear compartment. The trailer sports an articulated screen door that folds in the middle and canvas sides that allow meals to be prepared indoors during inclement weather. The Wild Goose version was featured as a rather complex build-it-yourself project in the April 1953 issue of Popular Mechanics magazine.

It's hard to estimate how many manufacturers there have been, but the number is certainly over one hundred. In recent years there has been a renewed interest in the tiny trailers, so much so that the supply of vintage units is far less than the demand. In response to the need, there are now over a dozen manufacturers of teardrop trailers and kits.

MOST PEOPLE AGREE that the first teardrop trailers were manufactured around 1933 or 1934. The Alpha Teardrop was probably made by a do-it-yourselfer with an eye to piecing together something functional yet stylish. Although the first teardrop trailer is probably long gone, the trailer pictured is certainly one of the earliest registered. The provenance of this homebuilt trailer is clear: it sports a California registration number of DMV872487, putting it at 1936. The wheels are from a 1935 Ford, while the fenders are from a mid-'30s Dodge pickup. The hitch is stamped "Fulton Type O Trailer Coupling, The Fulton CO, Milwaukee USA Patented Oct 1 1934." This hodgepodge of parts coupled with its 4 x 8-foot bed is exactly how a do-it-yourselfer would have built a trailer. Jerome Guffey purchased the trailer on eBay from a seller in Arcata, California. Guffey re-skinned the exterior with 1/8-inch mahogany plywood and reconfigured the galley to accommodate his wife's wicker collection. PHOTOGRAPHED AT ANTLERS RV PARK & CAMPGROUND, LAKEHEAD, CALIFORNIA.

THIS HOMEBUILT TRAILER has the bones of one of the very first teardrop trailers ever made. According to the owner of the trailer, Chris Hart, the trailer was built from plans featured in a two-part article titled "An Ideal Outdoorsman's Trailer" in the December 1936 and January 1937 issues of *Outdoor Life* magazine. The design of the trailer is credited to Walter Hille and J. S. McBeth of Los Angeles, who originally marketed the trailer under the Kaycraft Kampster name before the plans were published in *Outdoor Life*.

Chris found the trailer in Palm Springs, California, in almost unrestorable condition. He says that the original builder used the plans from *Outdoor Life* and, as was common at the time, adapted it to materials and parts available. The basic foundation of the trailer is a 4 x 10-foot piece of 3/4-inch plywood mounted on a steel frame. The top and sides of the trailer are also covered in plywood. Originally the plywood was covered with cotton batting for insulation and then topped with canvas. The aluminum was probably added at a later date. The restored trailer still has the original 1928–32 Chevrolet fenders and wheels, a 1935 Chevrolet truck center-mounted taillight, and the original pine drawers in the galley. Other parts were too far gone to restore, but rather than obtain new parts, Chris salvaged a number of parts, including additional taillights, interior light fixtures, interior paneling, and mirrors from a 1948 Zimmer trailer that was being scrapped. PHOTOGRAPHED AT GUAJOME COUNTY PARK, OCEANSIDE, CALIFORNIA.

THIS 1937 GYPSY CARAVAN is among the most stylish examples of the era. Manufactured by the Gypsy Caravan Company in Bell, California, it features the classic ovoid silhouette that earned these trailers their name. The trailer's exterior is finished in a padded artificial leather much like the DuPont Fabrikoid found on Glenn Curtiss's contemporary Aerocar Land Yacht. Standard automotive spoked wheels and wide whitewall tires complete a dapper little package. Fastidious care by a mere three owners during its lifetime has left this trailer in unrestored mint condition. The trailer is owned by Ann and Norm Markus. PHOTOGRAPHED AT ANTLERS RV PARK & CAMPGROUND, LAKEHEAD, CALIFORNIA.

THE DIMINUTIVE SIZE and modest cost of teardrops made them among the most popular trailer types offered as do-it-yourself kits. This example, probably built from plans found in the March/April 1939 issue of *Popular Homecraft* magazine, was completed in 1941. From the '30s through the '50s, "Build-Your-Own-Trailer" articles were also a staple of magazines such as *Popular Mechanics* and *Popular Science*. Moreover, the back pages of issues almost invariably featured advertisements for kit trailers and an array of stock trailer components. The trailer is owned by Steve and Candy Marino. PHOTOGRAPHED AT ANTLERS RV PARK & CAMPGROUND, LAKEHEAD, CALIFORNIA.

THIS DASHING TURQUOISE DUO consists of a 1929 Ford sedan delivery truck, dubbed the "Moonshine Express," and a 1940s Ken-Skill trailer named the "Hillbilly Bungalow." The vehicle has been beefed up with a Ford 302 engine and a new drive train. Owner Doug Cronn found the trailer at a private museum in Seattle, Washington, and persuaded the owner to part with it. He kept most of it original, including the windows, cabinet hardware, icebox, and genuine Port-O-Stove, which is fueled by a 1947 propane tank. The only major cosmetic changes besides the new paint scheme were the use of the same wheels as the tow vehicle and replacement of the original Chevrolet pickup taillights with Ford Model A taillights. **PHOTOGRAPHED AT THE DEMING LOG SHOW GROUNDS, BELLINGHAM, WASHINGTON.**

WHEN RICH AND MARY VOCK went looking for a classic car, they found this 1951 Ford Club Coupe at Memory Lanes in Wayne, Michigan. They also spied this teardrop and knew the pair had to be together. The 5 x 10-foot teardrop dating from 1943 bears the lettering "Harris Manufacturing, Stockton, California." The unique swooping profile suggests the trailer may have been homebuilt or manufactured in very limited production. PHOTOGRAPHED AT CAMP DEARBORN, MICHIGAN.

THE UNIVERSAL TRAILER COMPANY made this 5 x 9½-foot trailer under the Tourer and Tourette name in the 1940s. This restored trailer has the original icebox, stove, and cabinetry, although a few of the cabinet doors have been replaced. In response to the renewed popularity of teardrop trailers, a number of manufacturers are offering add-on rooms. The cabana-like combination changing room and dog house, which snaps onto the side of the trailer, is constructed from an EZ-Up display frame and canvas especially tailored to the owner's specifications. The trailer is owned by Rando and Lori Thyr. **PHOTOGRAPHED AT GUAJOME COUNTY PARK, OCEANSIDE, CALIFORNIA.**

THE MOST BASIC DESIGN for a teardrop trailer is well illustrated in this 1946 Kit trailer. The trailer's body is constructed on a standard-issue 4 x 8-foot sheet of plywood. When Craig and Patti Holroyd found the Kit in a backyard in Long Beach, California, the little trailer was slowly melting into the ground. It was in such bad shape that it couldn't be towed, and they had to lift its carcass onto a flatbed trailer. The couple slowly nursed the wee trailer back to life by adding a new fiberglass skin and oak paneling on the interior and by totally refurbishing the galley. Patti says that the question most people ask is, "Can you really sleep in that thing?" to which she comments, "It's just a matter of allocating your two feet of space. Once you've established your territory, you're good to go." The tow vehicle is a 1962 Rambler Classic Station Wagon with its original 195.7-cubic-inch, six-cylinder engine. PHOTOGRAPHED AT GUAJOME COUNTY PARK, OCEANSIDE, CALIFORNIA.

THIS IS THE ONLY 1949 Streamline Aero Chief currently registered on the West Coast. Owners Damian and Sandra Rutherford, founders of the Spamboree, a teardrop and vintage trailer rally, say that it was probably built in a small shop somewhere in Vermont and sold through an adjacent car dealership. Other offerings from the company included a smaller version of the Aero Chief named the Aero Maiden and a smaller one still, the Papoose.

The galley has the original configuration, but some pieces have had to be replaced due to the effects of age. It is well equipped with vintage items from the couple's collection and an ever-growing assortment of flea market finds. The Aero Chief's cabin is an ample (at least by teardrop standards) 5 feet 1 inch wide x 9 feet 6 inches long and has plenty of cargo space; one compartment is cleverly tucked beneath the full-size bed. PHOTOGRAPHED AT GUA-JOME COUNTY PARK, OCEANSIDE, CALIFORNIA.

SMOKEY BEAR (facing) presides over a 1947 Modernistic teardrop, whose gleaming skin of Kaiser aluminum looks about as old as tomorrow. Unlike Masonite-bodied trailers, which quickly fall to pieces if not properly maintained, aluminum-skinned units can take years of neglect and still be returned to near-new condition—albeit through generous applications of elbow grease. PHOTOGRAPHED AT ANTLERS RV PARK & CAMPGROUND, LAKEHEAD, CALIFORNIA.

TRAILORBOAT ENGINEERING of San Rafael produced these clever little trailers (above) from 1961 to 1964. During those three years, less than five hundred were produced and are highly sought after today. The interior houses two cozy campers; the rear galley has ample storage space, and a bar above the hitch is fashioned to accommodate an outboard motor. The tow vehicle is a 1954 Cadillac convertible. Both are owned by Steven Katkowsky. PHOTOGRAPHED BY STEVE KATKOWSKY IN SAN RAFAEL, CALIFORNIA.

IN 2005, Jim Eddy found this 1947 Tourette trailer (below) in a woman's backyard in Wyoming, Michigan. The trailer had a 1961 license plate, so it ostensibly had not moved since 1961. The owner also had the original registration dating from 1948. Most of the interior had rotted out and much of the galley was rusted and oxidized. Eddy saw potential for a restoration and purchased the trailer. Inside the trailer he found a roll of canvas and discovered that it was the original awning. Miraculously, the awning was in great condition. All Eddy had to do was replace the plastic window and repair a few tears. Tourettes were manufactured in Kansas City, Missouri. PHOTOGRAPHED AT CAMP DEARBORN, MICHIGAN.

THE 1956 KOM-PAK Sportsman echoed the Trailorboat's ingenious configuration but also boasted a rakish fiberglass body better suited to the automotive styling of the period. The industrial use of fiberglass advanced steadily after World War II; in 1953, the Chevrolet Corvette became the first American production car to use the tough, lightweight, and rustproof composite for all major body panels. Camping vehicles, with their demand for both strength and lightness, were another natural application for fiberglass technology. Fiberglass was also much cheaper than formed or stamped steel where limited numbers of complex shapes were required—an important advantage for the small production runs typical of the recreational vehicle industry. The tow vehicle, which has no problem pulling the trailer at highway speeds, is a 1956 Cadillac Sedan DeVille. The stylish duet is owned by Phil and Esther Harmon. PHOTO-GRAPHED AT THE DEMING LOG SHOW GROUNDS, BELLINGHAM, WASHINGTON.

THIS 1936 FORD TRUCK made from new parts (above) tows a rare 1955 Benroy teardrop trailer. Owner Cullen Tate got the Benroy in a trade from the previous owner in Southfield, Michigan, who was using it as yard art. PHOTOGRAPHED AT CAMP DEARBORN, MICHIGAN.

THIS STRIKING WOODY COMBO (below) consists of a 10 x 4-foot 1948 homebuilt trailer towed by a 1940 Ford woody. Cliff Parker, the duo's owner, restored both vehicles to showstopping quality. The trailer, which was said to have been built from plans published in a *Popular Mechanics* magazine, originally had an aluminum skin. Cliff "glued and screwed" 1/8-inch ribbon-grain mahogany panels and maple trim directly over the aluminum. He topped the trailer with the same vinyl material as the woody. Cliff was able to restore the maple trim on the automobile but had to replace the body panels—a feat he accomplished by using the same ribbon-grain mahogany as the trailer. PHOTOGRAPHED AT GUAJOME COUNTY PARK, OCEANSIDE, CALIFORNIA.

THE KAMP MASTER was an unusual teardrop-derived design whose mammoth rear hatch opened to form a full-height camping trailer by way of cleverly designed canvas flies. In addition to its full-height door, the Kamp Master featured a teardrop-style hatch that opened into the sleeping compartment. Aimed at outdoorsmen, the trailer boasted a leather-lined interior with plenty of cupboard and closet space as well as a rod and gun shelf.

The partially deployed Kamp Master (facing) shows the canvas flies—replaceable with mosquito netting in warm weather—and the full-height door. The sleeping compartment, just visible through the open front hatch, could be used with the trailer in either the stowed or deployed position. Thanks to a weight of only 840 pounds, the unit required no trailer brakes and imposed a relatively light ninety-four-pound tongue load on the tow vehicle, avoiding the need for overload springs. Moreover, its streamlined shape was said to reduce drag by some two hundred pounds at sixty miles per hour, as compared to conventional rectangular trailers. The Kamp Master's manufacturer, King's Trailer Company, billed its aluminum skin as a "Life-time" finish—a claim this example dating from 1950 seems to bear out. The trailer is owned by Mike and Debbie Smith. PHOTO-GRAPHED AT ANTLERS RV PARK & CAMPGROUND, LAKEHEAD, CALIFORNIA.

PHYLLIS AND JOHN GREEN found this 1950 Kamp Master trailer (above) in Ukiah, California, thanks to a tip from fellow trailerite Wayne Fergusson. An extraordinary find, this trailer is all original, thanks to careful storage by the previous owner who purchased it in 1955. When the Kamp Master is buttoned down for the road, it has a 6 x 10-foot footprint and is only 4 feet high. When configured for camping, the interior has over 6 feet of headroom. The original awning combined with the original skirt provide an additional room. The tow vehicle is a 1949 Chevrolet five-window pickup. PHOTOGRAPHED AT THE ANTLERS RV PARK & CAMPGROUND, LAKEHEAD, CALIFORNIA.

DURING THE LATE 1930S and through the 1940s, many popular handyman magazines published articles and plans for teardrop trailers. Some small fabrication and auto body shops, especially those located near aircraft manufacturers, tried their hand at building teardrop trailers. Such is the case with this very unusual teardrop first spied by Ed Kelson at a swap meet.

It was very large for a teardrop trailer: 6 feet wide, 5 feet high, and 13 feet long. The trailer was a mixture of parts from other vehicles, including a teardrop-shaped hitch stamped "Acme Manufacturing November 17th, 1939" and Ford Model A axle and springs. The body appeared to have been made by someone familiar with aircraft welding and fabrication principles, perhaps someone employed at the nearby Boeing Aircraft facility. Additional evidence that it was made in an aircraft facility comes from the unusually large, curved Plexiglas window that takes up a significant part of the front panel of the trailer. Plexiglas was first introduced in the United States in 1936 and was used in aircraft windshields, gun turrets, and canopies.

The paint scheme was entirely Ed's idea and is in what can best be described as a retro-1960s, San Francisco flower-power scheme with a twenty-first-century flair. The tow vehicle is a 1948 Ford panel truck on a 1978 T-Bird frame. PHOTOGRAPHED ON THE BANKS OF THE NOOKSACK RIVER NEAR NUGENTS CORNER, WASHINGTON.

THIS TEARDROP was built from the ground up by Rod Glassett. Rod wanted to build a 5 x 10-foot teardrop trailer as lightweight as a 4 x 8-foot teardrop he had built fifteen years previously. He achieved that goal by starting with an aluminum frame and using plywood sheathing one size smaller than usual. The trailer weighs in at 950 pounds dry and can easily be towed with any vehicle. The trailer's galley contains a microwave oven, refrigerator, water tank, and fully extendable pull-out counters to accommodate a stove and provide additional counter space. The counter workspace is made of marble. Twin speakers are set into the galley's lid and provide soothing sounds to the chef as he prepares sumptuous repasts. The exterior of the trailer is coated in Rhinohide, a durable sprayed-on material that is usually reserved for pickup truck beds. The fenders came from the R. W. Johnson Company of Auburn, California, which makes fenders specially tailored for teardrop trailers. A crowning touch is provided by twin teardrop-shaped taillights and teardrop-shaped porch lights. PHOTOGRAPHED AT THE DEMING LOG SHOW GROUNDS, BELLINGHAM, WASHINGTON.

THIS WOODSY TEARDROP was built from the bottom up by Bill Eosel of Port Sydney, Ontario, Canada. It's towed by a 1948 Pontiac Streamliner Deluxe with a 248-cubic-inch Straight 8 and a four-speed Hydromatic transmission. A rarity for teardrops, this trailer sports a bathroom complete with shower, which pops up from the black steel box on the front of the trailer. The streamlined combo is owned by Allan Woods of Ontario, Canada. **PHOTOGRAPHED AT CAMP DEARBORN, MICHIGAN.**

THIS SPANISH BLUE COMBO is owned by Ed Avila. The teardrop trailer was built in 1996 but was modeled on a 1946 Kit trailer design. The tow vehicle is a 1949 Chevrolet pickup. PHOTOGRAPHED AT THE DEMING LOG SHOW GROUNDS, BELLINGHAM, WASHINGTON.

MASTER TEARDROP BUILDER and trailer restorer Rod Glassett built this stunning coal black teardrop trailer (facing, above) for Ken Masden. Ken wanted a trailer to complement his 1936 Ford three-window coupe, so Rod constructed the trailer to mirror the curvy profile of the automobile. Ken and his wife, Marty, are avid teardrop fans, so much so that they host an annual Fourth of July teardrop event, the Carnation Rally, on their farm in Carnation, Washington. PHOTOGRAPHED AT THE DEMING LOG SHOW GROUNDS, BELLINGHAM, WASHINGTON.

STEVE AND PEGGY BIRLEY are often the hit of RV campgrounds when they arrive in their 1928 Ford Model A (facing, below) with their home-built teardrop in tow. The Model A is all original,

including its 40 horsepower engine. The Model A was Steve's first car. He purchased it in 1962 while attending high school in Mossyrock, Washington. PHOTOGRAPHED AT THE DEMING LOG SHOW GROUNDS, BELLINGHAM, WASHINGTON.

THANKS TO their lightweight design, teardrop trailers can be towed with almost any vehicle. Wendy and Steven Hughes-Jelen use a 2003 Mini Cooper (above) painted in a jaunty British Racing Green to tow this new teardrop trailer. The trailer is made by Ed Ester of Seattle, Washington, who has taken his skills as a cabinetmaker and applied them to what is essentially a cabinet on wheels. PHOTOGRAPHED AT THE DEMING LOG SHOW GROUNDS, BELLINGHAM, WASHINGTON.

IN 2006, Douglas Hoder of Camino, California, built this 4-foot 6-inch x 10-foot teardrop from the ground up. An Arts and Crafts–style enthusiast, Hoder detailed the trim in what can only be described as an homage to the Arts and Crafts style. The wood panels are a mixture of birch and maple. The trim is executed in mahogany. Hoder used stainless steel in the galley and skinned the trailer in aluminum. The ample interior, which also has Arts and Crafts accents, is guarded by Daizy the Wonderdog. PHOTOGRAPHED AT THE ANTLERS RV PARK & CAMPGROUND, LAKEHEAD, CALIFORNIA.

TEARDROP TRAILERS are often canvasses to demonstrate their owners' skills and passion. Dan Hazard, who makes his living as a videographer, was trained as a machinist. His skill in working with metal is evident in all aspects of what he calls his "work in progress teardrop." The 5 x 10-foot trailer (facing) has an 18-inch extension for a cleverly placed generator that provides power for a microwave and air conditioner, resulting in what is one of the rare teardrops with AC. Certainly the most striking aspect of his creation is the swirled finish, which he created by mounting a grinder on its side, affixing sandpaper to the grinder's wheel, and fashioning a jig on a horizontal bar. The ample galley, constructed of oak with mahogany accents, folds out to 10 feet. It is the creation of woodworker Charlie Hanson. PHOTOGRAPHED AT THE ANTLERS RV PARK & CAMPGROUND, LAKE-HEAD, CALIFORNIA.

LARRY GRIM constructed this homebuilt teardrop (above) and truly followed the homebuilt teardrop aesthetic. One day while Larry was wandering through the woods of a cemetery, he found the suspension and wheels of a 1935 Ford tangled in the weeds. He extricated the frame and sandblasted it and the wire wheels. Then, guided by plans he found in a September 1947 issue of *Mechanix Illustrated* magazine, he constructed the trailer. The tow vehicle is a pheasant red 1947 Ford that had 45,000 original miles when he purchased it. PHOTOGRAPHED AT CAMP DEAR-BORN, MICHIGAN.

TEARDROP TRAILERS are in such demand that a handful of enthusiasts have taken to manufacturing their own trailers. Grant Whipp manufacturers the Li'l Bear Tag-Alongs in Redding, California. The 4 x 8-foot trailer is modeled on the Kit trailer, which was manufactured from mid-1945 until mid-1948. The Li'l Bear comes completely assembled for approximately $6,750. PHOTOGRAPHED AT THE ANTLERS RV PARK & CAMPGROUND, LAKEHEAD, CALIFORNIA.

THIS CUSTOM 5 x 9-foot teardrop trailer was designed and built by David Nathenson and Louise Stein. The couple, who are avid off-roaders, wanted something they could take on their adventures without the risk of damaging the trailer or hampering their progress as they explored the wilds. The trailer, which they call the Daggett after the location of the first teardrop trailer they ever saw, was designed from the ground up.

The first order of business to make the trailer off-road worthy was to place the trailer body well above the axle to create a high center with 15 inches of clearance. Of equal importance was to make the trailer easily follow the Jeep through any terrain, a task accomplished with the aid of a "lock and roll" hitch configured much like a universal joint. Shock absorbers and brakes were added and 1-inch plywood was used on all the major panels. **PHOTOGRAPHED AT GUAJOME COUNTY PARK, OCEANSIDE, CALIFORNIA.**

TEARDROP TRAILERS, because of their diminutive stature, lend themselves to personal interpretations. Dean Tennis, who retired from a job at aircraft manufacturer Rohr, Inc., in Chula Vista, California, put his years of aircraft design experience to work when he built the "Chummy" teardrop trailer. Tennis had originally intended to build a small camper by building a small boat, which he would then turn upside down, elevate with a system of poles, and then outfit with canvas sides. This contraption would serve as both a boat and a shelter. After pondering the possibilities for a while, he realized he really didn't like boating at all and preferred motoring and camping. Nevertheless, his pondering came to good use when he was able to apply the same building techniques to this unique trailer.

The Chummy's skin is 1/8-inch oak plywood fastened to a system of pine ribs, much like the fuselage of an airplane. The top is sheathed in a Naugahyde-like material that is used in convertible tops. The trim is also oak. The lightweight aircraft-type design results in a trailer that weighs less than four hundred pounds. Rather than employ the traditional trunk-like galley of other teardrops, Tennis elected to devise a system of drawers and pullout shelves for the galley. The wheels of the Chummy match those of the all-original 1930 Ford Town Sedan. **PHOTOGRAPHED AT GUAJOME COUNTY PARK, OCEANSIDE, CALIFORNIA.**

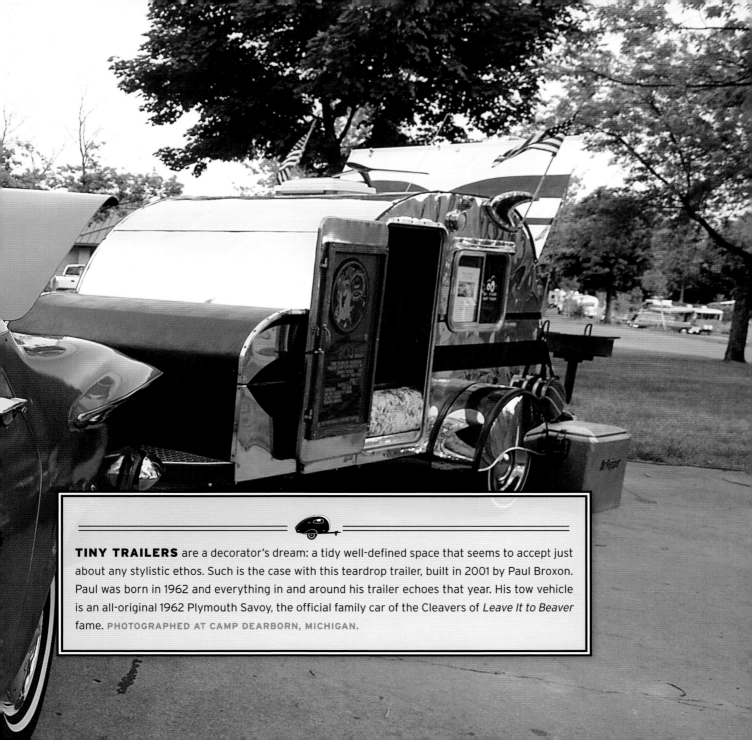

TINY TRAILERS are a decorator's dream: a tidy well-defined space that seems to accept just about any stylistic ethos. Such is the case with this teardrop trailer, built in 2001 by Paul Broxon. Paul was born in 1962 and everything in and around his trailer echoes that year. His tow vehicle is an all-original 1962 Plymouth Savoy, the official family car of the Cleavers of *Leave It to Beaver* fame. **PHOTOGRAPHED AT CAMP DEARBORN, MICHIGAN.**

JOE BOSIER used his skills as a technical illustrator when he designed and built this woodstrip teardrop trailer in 2005. Bosier had previously built a woodstrip canoe using plans from an early 1990s issue of *Popular Mechanics* magazine. The inspiration to build the 10¹/₂ x 4¹/₂-foot trailer came from a teardrop trailer he saw at an old car show. He purchased an axle and then constructed a steel frame. His father, John Bosier, machined all the cedar strips in his woodshop, and father and son constructed the trailer together. **PHOTO-GRAPHED AT CAMP DEARBORN, MICHIGAN.**

A TINY 1958 Nash Metropolitan owned by Rhonda Gelstein is a perfect vehicle for this 3½ x 5-foot Dew Drop cargo trailer made by Cullen Tate. Tate had previously owned a classic mid-1950s Benroy trailer and used it as inspiration for the Dew Drop. **PHOTOGRAPHED AT CAMP DEARBORN, MICHIGAN.**

ONE OF THE MOST spectacular new teardrop trailers is this 2006 Ultra Model 550 Camp-Inn trailer customized by owner Doug Hardekopf. The 5 x 10-foot trailer is equipped with satellite television, a furnace, air conditioning, an eight-gallon water tank, an eight-gallon gray water tank, electric brakes, and a Fan-Tastic roof vent. The tow vehicle is a 2003 New Volkswagen Beetle convertible. Along for the ride are Tom and Mary Bamborough (in the front seat) and Al Hesselbart (in green shirt). Doug Hardekopf graciously allowed Mary to drive. PHOTOGRAPHED AT CAMP DEARBORN, MICHIGAN.

THIS TRAILER is a cross between a canned ham and a teardrop trailer. It appears to have been built in the late 1930s by West Coast Body Builders in Willamette, Oregon. Owners Jerry and Jenean Marlette found it moldering away in a field in Lewiston, Idaho, where it had served as a shed for twenty-five years. When the photograph was taken, most of the 14 x 6-foot interior had been gutted in preparation for restoration. The tow vehicle is a 1960 Chevrolet Bel Air. PHOTOGRAPHED AT THE DEMING LOG SHOW GROUNDS, BELLING-HAM, WASHINGTON.

CANNED HAM
Trailers

ALMOST FROM THE DAY THAT NEWFANGLED MOTORCARS STARTED

rolling down the road, clever folks figured out ways to hitch up a temporary

home on wheels. The first travel trailers were understandably boxy affairs built

by carpenters with little more than a hammer and saw. The first mainstream

manufactured trailers, built in the late 1920s by Arthur Sherman's Covered Wagon

Trailer Company, still held to the angular profile. But by the early 1930s, fueled by

the streamlining craze and more competition from multiple trailer manufacturers,

a new style of trailer emerged.

This new style, which was basically an elongated top stretched over two oval sides, was a sharp departure from the clunky styles of the '20s. At the time, most folks referred to these trailers as teardrop style, a designation that was later usurped by smaller trailers with an aft external kitchen. The original teardrops became known as canned ham or ham can trailers because of the uncanny resemblance to a metal ham container. Because of its economi-

cal construction (no compound curves like those seen in Airstream-like trailers), the canned ham style endures to this day. It is fairly easy to date these trailers just by external observation: generally the curvier the trailer, the older it is. As

time went on, trailer manufacturers learned that it was a lot easier fitting cabinets and other interior accessories into a squarish shape rather than a curve.

PATRICK EWING found this 1951 13-foot Comet trailer (facing), manufactured in Wichita, Kansas, in a dilapidated garage in Coupeville, Washington. After extracting the trailer from its longtime nest, he sold it to Sandy Smelser. And none too soon, for a few weeks later the garage slid into Puget Sound during a ferocious storm. Because the trailer had been sheltered for so many years, little major restoration was necessary inside or out. The Comet is posed with a 1940 burgundy Chevrolet two-door sedan by owner Rod Glassett, especially modified to tow trailers. PHOTOGRAPHED AT THE DEMING LOG SHOW GROUNDS, BELLINGHAM, WASHINGTON.

The interior of the trailer was amazingly intact. The only significant repair work that needed to be done was a bit of refurbishment to the original warm-toned birch paneling. The stove and the Astral refrigerator are original to the trailer and required little more than a cleaning to get them up and running. Most amazing is the original covered-wagon-themed upholstery and vintage linoleum flooring. Sandy took her decorating cues from the dinette's fabric and continued the western theme throughout the trailer. She's quick to point out that almost all the accessories are vintage.

THIS 1955 COMET TRAILER began its life in Wichita, Kansas, and eventually wound up serving as a hunting blind in northern Michigan. Michelle and Ken Defer spied it one day, loved its retro styling, and extricated it from its woody mooring. They began a "frame off" three-year restoration in 2003. All the wood and aluminum was replaced, but the couple was able to refurbish the original hardware. The result of their hard work is simply stunning. **PHOTOGRAPHED AT CAMP DEARBORN, MICHIGAN.**

WHILE TRAILER INTERIORS of the late 1950s generally followed domestic trends, exterior styling was heavily influenced by the era's flamboyant automotive designs. Integrated two-tone paint schemes first appeared on cars during the early '50s; by 1955, virtually every make offered two-tone or even three-tone paint jobs, usually defined by some form of rakish side trim. Wraparound windshields and backlights had also been widely adopted by 1955 and quickly became an emblem of automotive modernity. Trailer manufacturers did their best to echo such features after their own fashion: this 1957 Comet trailer, with its glass-cornered "wraparound windshield" and two-toned action lines, echoes the classic styling of the 1957 Chevrolet Bel Air tow car. The trailer and car are owned by Duke and Fay Waldrop. PHOTOGRAPHED IN WINTER HAVEN, FLORIDA.

THIS SWEET DUO, a 1955 Dodge C3 Town Panel truck and a 1954 12-foot Zollinger Va-Ka-Shun-Ette is painted in that oh-so-'50s color combination of sea foam green and antique white. Va-Ka-Shun-Ette trailers were made in Elkhart, Indiana. Shannon and Cecily Near purchased the duo in 2004 and did all the restoration. PHOTOGRAPHED AT CAMP DEARBORN, MICHIGAN.

EVEN MORE VIBRANT interior colors arrived in the late 1950s, paralleling the fashion for vividly colored automobiles. The Comet (facing) features vinyl banquettes color keyed to the laminated plastic panels in the cabinet doors, while the drain board uses a contrasting plastic laminate material edged in bright metal, as was customary until the early 1960s. The checkered floor and stove cover are a modern addition by the owner.

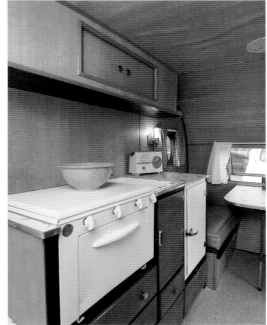

THE SLEEK PROFILE of this 16-foot 1955 Holly is ahead of its time. Although large house trailers in the mid-1950s usually sported an angular profile, most canned ham trailers still utilized the classic oval shape. By the late 1960s, most of them lost their curves and gradually transitioned to the nondescript white boxes that are seen today. The Holly's interior is lined in honey-toned birch plywood, a material that remained in most canned ham trailers well into the 1960s. The trailer is owned by Wendy Case and Ross Westerbur. **PHOTOGRAPHED AT CAMP DEARBORN, MICHIGAN.**

Shasta

FOUNDED IN 1941 BY CALIFORNIAN ROBERT GRAY, SHASTA INDUSTRIES CLAIMED TO BE THE OLDEST **CONTINUOUS** TRAILER MANUFACTURER IN AMERICA UNTIL COACHMEN INDUSTRIES RETIRED THE BRAND IN 2004. THE VENERABLE AIRSTREAM TRAILER, FIRST MANUFACTURED IN 1936, WILL SOON TAKE THE CONTINUOUS MANUFACTURING CROWN. (AIRSTREAM WENT ON A PRODUCTION HIATUS DURING WORLD WAR II AND RESTARTED IN THE LATE 1940S.) THE FIRST TRAILERS ROLLED OUT BY SHASTA INDUSTRIES WERE BOXY BREAD-LOAF-STYLE TRAILERS NAMED COZY CRUISERS, BUILT FOR WARTIME HOUSING. THIS TYPE OF TRAILER WAS KNOWN AS A COMMITTEE TRAILER SINCE IT WAS DESIGNED BY A COMMITTEE OF TRAILER MANUFACTURERS SPECIFICALLY FOR TEMPORARY AND MOVABLE HOUSING. SINCE THEIR EXTERIORS WERE USUALLY SHEATHED IN LESS-THAN-DURABLE MASONITE, HOMASOTE, AND PLYWOOD, FEW OF THE COMMITTEE TRAILERS SURVIVE TODAY. AFTER THE WAR, COZY CRUISERS ACQUIRED AN ALUMINUM SKIN AND WERE MANUFACTURED BY SHASTA INDUSTRIES UNDER THE AUSPICES OF THE

COZY CRUISER TRAILER COMPANY. THE LAST COZY CRUISERS WERE MANUFACTURED IN EARLY 1952. BY LATE 1952, THE COMPANY HAD TRANSITIONED TO THE SHASTA NAME. ADVERTISEMENTS FOR SHASTAS NOTED THAT THEY WERE "FORMERLY COZY CRUISER."

THE EARLIEST CANNED-HAM-STYLE TRAILER SPORTING THE SHASTA NAME APPEARS TO BE THE 1400 (PRESUMABLY 14 FEET LONG), FOLLOWED BY THE 1500 AND 1600. SHASTA INDUSTRIES ALSO MANUFACTURED HOUSE TRAILERS WITH A RAKED PROFILE UP TO 35 FEET IN LENGTH. OVER THE NEXT TWENTY YEARS SHASTA INTRODUCED A NUMBER OF MODELS, INCLUDING THE 12½-FOOT COMPACT, THREE 16-FOOT MODELS NAMED THE AIRFLYTE, ASTRODOME, AND ASTROFLYTE, AND A 20-FOOT MODEL SIMPLY NAMED THE TWENTY. IN THE 1960S, THE SHASTA WAS THE BEST-SELLING TRAILER IN AMERICA. BY 1973, THERE WERE CLOSE TO FIVE HUNDRED DEALERS WHO SOLD SHASTAS. THE SHASTA NAME COULD BE FOUND ON SMALL CAMPING-STYLE TRAILERS, LARGER FIFTH-WHEELS, AND EVEN MOTORHOMES. ALL OF THE SMALLER TRAILERS HAD SIMILAR CONFIGURATIONS AS OTHER CANNED-HAM-STYLE TRAILERS OF THE TIME. BUT WHAT REALLY SEPARATED THE SHASTA TRAILER FROM THE CROWD WAS ITS DISTINCTIVE WINGS, MUCH COVETED BY COLLECTORS. THESE SPIFFY APPENDAGES WERE ADDED TO THE AFT OF THE SHASTAS IN THE LATE 1950S. THEIR COMPOSITION AND SIZE CHANGED A BIT OVER THE YEARS. BY THE EARLY 1970S, THE DISTINCTIVE WINGS HAD BEEN SIGNIFICANTLY REDUCED IN SIZE. BY THE MID 1980S, MUCH TO THE DISTRESS OF SHASTA LOVERS, THEY WERE LOST ENTIRELY.

COACHMEN INDUSTRIES OF ELKHART, INDIANA, BOUGHT SHASTA IN 1976 AND RECONFIGURED THE LOGO AND THE TRAILERS. THEY ALSO EXPANDED THE LINE BY ADDING TENT TRAILERS, PARK MODELS, AND LARGER MOTORHOMES. BUT AFTER THE WINGS WERE ABANDONED, SHASTAS STARTED TO LOOK LIKE OTHER TRAILERS, AND THE TINY TOASTERS LOOKED AS IF THEY WOULD FADE INTO THE SUNSET. BUT THANKS TO A RENAISSANCE IN VINTAGE TRAILERS THAT STARTED IN THE 1990S, MORE AND MORE SHASTAS ARE BEING COAXED ONTO THE ROAD AFTER BEING DISCOVERED TUCKED IN BARNS AND GARAGES AND MOLDING AWAY IN BACKYARDS AND PASTURES.

THE SHASTA IS ONE OF THE MOST COLLECTED VINTAGE CANNED HAM TRAILERS. A NUMBER OF WEB SITES AND GROUPS CATER TO SHASTA AFICIONADOS' NEEDS. FIND THEM IN THE RESOURCE SECTION OF THIS BOOK.

FACTORY VERSIONS of the Shasta trailer are painted, usually in a two-tone theme. When Luke Hinman, an engineer from Boeing in Seattle, restored this 12-foot 1962 Shasta (facing) from the ground up, he just couldn't bear to paint the newly fabricated skin. PHOTOGRAPHED AT THE DEMING LOG SHOW GROUNDS IN BELLINGHAM, WASHINGTON.

A JAUNTY TWO-TONE SCHEME enlivens this 15-foot 1957 Shasta (facing, below). The zig-zag action line on the trailer's corrugated sides gamely emulates the tailfins that were all the rage in automotive designs of the mid-to-late 1950s; the V-motif at the rear was yet another favorite styling theme of the era. The tow car is a 1956 Chevrolet Bel Air, one of the best-selling cars of the decade. The combo is owned by Gerry Hagelund. PHOTOGRAPHED AT THE DEMING LOG SHOW GROUNDS, BELLINGHAM, WASHINGTON.

FOLLOWING A QUARTER CENTURY of subdued wood-toned interiors, strident colors finally found their way into trailers during the mid-1950s, influenced by the mainstream arrival of modern art. Meanwhile, cabinetwork emulated the contemporary trends found in homes. The postwar era saw the rise of the ubiquitous California rancher, a home style featuring simple lines and rustic materials such as brick, stained wood, wrought iron, and copper. However, entirely new materials also appeared in ranchers; among them

were laminated plastic countertops sold under brand names such as Micarta and Formica, which offered a virtually infinite range of pattern and color possibilities. The Shasta's interior features splashes of bright yellow in the laminated plastic center panels of the overhead storage cabinets as well as in the upholstery of the dining booth. The wig-wag pattern surrounding the panels was another popular rancher motif of the late '50s.

THIS 1956 SHASTA is towed by a mechanically original 1947 Canadian Pontiac with a flat-head six-cylinder engine. The only modifications to the vehicle were lowering it a couple of inches and adding flame-orange metallic paint. The trailer, which is painted with the same paint scheme, is 12 x 6 feet. The Shasta was a ground-up restoration; it has new electrical wiring, plumbing, and insulation, and was reframed. The trailer and car are owned by Lew and Lesley Puls. PHOTOGRAPHED AT THE DEMING LOG SHOW GROUNDS, BELLINGHAM, WASHINGTON.

WHEN IT CAME TIME to decorate the trailer (facing and previous spread), Lesley Puls jumped to the task. She says she heard that a woman designed the Shasta interior and she tends to agree, since there is lots of storage space. Lesley decided to decorate the trailer in a soda fountain theme (facing). She installed the fabric first and let the rest of the interior take its cues from the style and color scheme of the fabric. She explains that she wanted to create something a little different, something that echoed the carefree times of the 1950s. "I wanted a happy-looking place," she explained. "Something colorful, cheery, and bright." Indeed, by the mid- to late 1950s, trailer manufacturers, like interior and furniture designers, were shifting from predominately neutrals and adding bright and bold splashes of color.

The dinette converts into a bed that is large enough to accommodate a couple of children. There is even a canopy above the master bed that can be used for additional sleeping accommodations. When absolutely necessary, the tidy little trailer can sleep five.

THIS TWO-TONE 1957 Shasta (above) owned by Keith and Barb Thompson is teamed up with a 1955 Ford F100 owned by Charles Taylor. PHOTOGRAPHED AT THE DEMING LOG SHOW GROUNDS, BELLINGHAM, WASHINGTON.

TINY TRAILERS like this winged 12½-foot 1963 Shasta (facing, above) make great foils to highlight one's memorabilia collection. Vintage trailer rallies often have theme nights where attendees are encouraged to light up their homes on wheels. The trailer is owned by Gary and Sally Lodholm. PHOTOGRAPHED AT THE DEMING LOG SHOW GROUNDS, BELLINGHAM, WASHINGTON.

RIGHT OUT of the canned ham mold comes this 1959 14-foot (12-foot body) Fan trailer (facing, below). Fans were built in Wakarusa, Indiana, a stone's throw south of Elkhart, Indiana, the modern-day trailer capital of the world. The bicycle in the foreground is a sturdy 1948 Schwinn that, in a former life, served as a delivery vehicle for the *Elkhart Truth* newspaper. The trailer is owned by Bill Walter and Lori Osborne. PHOTOGRAPHED AT CAMP DEARBORN, MICHIGAN.

THIS 1954 Hanson Love Bug (below) illustrates precisely why this style of trailer is called a canned ham. Love Bug was built in Glendora, California, not far from the terminus of fabled Route 66. Packed into its 14-foot (tongue-to-bumper) body is sleeping for six (there is a bunk over the convertible dinette), a four-burner stove, and an icebox. The trailer is owned by Robin and Kevin Ramos. Robin holds the distinction of being the grand prizewinner at the 2006 Spamboree for her flavorful meat product creation. PHOTOGRAPHED AT GUAJOME COUNTY PARK, OCEANSIDE, CALIFORNIA.

THIS 16-FOOT West Coast Trailer manufactured by Westfield Inc. of Los Angeles was restored by Dayton Taylor. Dayton owns and operates Vintagetrailercrazy.com. At any one time, Taylor usually has a couple of trailers for sale and is in the process of restoring others. The West Coast is towed by a 1941 Lincoln Zephyr with suicide doors, so called because their reverse opening would catch the wind and hold them open, thus enabling passengers to easily jump out or be pushed out. Or, more likely, there was the perceived danger that either the doors could be accidentally torn off if they were opened at high speed or the door of a parked car could be accidentally bumped by a vehicle approaching from the rear and cause great damage to an exiting passenger. PHOTOGRAPHED AT GUAJOME COUNTY PARK, OCEANSIDE, CALIFORNIA.

THIS QUINTESSENTIAL canned ham trailer is owned by Tammy Fuller, a member of a group of adventurous fly-fishing women called Sisters on the Fly (Tammy is sister #119). All of the women have vintage trailers, and great pains are taken to decorate the trailers in outdoorsy themes. (Check the resource section of this book for more information on the group.) Tammy's trailer is a 1957 Aljo manufactured in Alhambra, California. She acquired it in early 2005 after her previous trailer was rear-ended on the highway. **PHOTOGRAPHED AT THE DEMING LOG SHOW GROUNDS, BELLINGHAM, WASHINGTON.**

TAMMY DECORATED the tidy 12½ x 6-foot interior in what she describes as "cowgirl kitsch." She named the trailer Miss Montana as an homage to cherubic-faced cowgirl singer Patsy Montana, who is most noted for the song "I Want to Be a Cowboy's Sweetheart." Highlights of the cowgirl-decorating theme (most of them flea market finds) include rodeo memorabilia, vintage national park brochures, and pennants and decals from Miss Montana's travels.

AS THE VINTAGE TRAILER phenomenon becomes increasingly popular, more and more owners are viewing their trailer and tow vehicle as a custom set. This 1960 12-foot Aero trailer built in Elkhart, Indiana, and its tow vehicle, a custom-built 1956 Lincoln station wagon, is a stunning example of the phenomenon. Owner Phil Schaeffer of Indianapolis, Indiana, bought the trailer at an IRS auction of a taxi company. The trailer was being used as a break room, so it was in relatively good mechanical condition, although it needed a lot of cosmetic work. The pièce de résistance of the duo is the tow vehicle, which is a modified 1956 Lincoln Sedan. Phil thought a station wagon would look better than a regular sedan, so he drew up a set of plans and had the Carolina Rod Shop of Greenville, South Carolina, do the customizing. The result is a 20-foot 9-inch station wagon (extended 14 inches from the original). PHOTOGRAPHED AT CAMP DEARBORN, MICHIGAN.

Serro Scotty

ONE OF THE MOST ESTEEMED AND COLLECTED TINY TRAILERS IS THE SERRO SCOTTY. ACCORDING TO THE COMPANY, IT WAS BORN IN JULY 1956 WHEN RETIRED CAR SALESMAN JOHN SERRO WENT ON A WEEKEND FISHING TRIP TO MARYLAND. ALAS, WHEN HE ARRIVED AT THE CABIN, IT WAS POURING RAIN. APPARENTLY A FAIR-WEATHER ANGLER, SERRO MOPED AROUND BECAUSE HE DIDN'T WANT TO FISH DURING THE DELUGE. AFTER A TIME, SERRO SKETCHED OUT A DESIGN ON THE BACK OF A CALENDAR FOR A TIDY 13-FOOT TRAILER. PREVIOUSLY, SERRO HAD DESIGNED AND BUILT A 16 1/2-FOOT TRAILER IN HIS GARAGE, WHICH HE HAD NO SUCCESS MARKETING. SERRO ALSO PRODUCED A COUPLE OF HUNDRED 10-FOOT TEARDROP TRAILERS HE NAMED THE SPORTSMAN JR. BUT IT WAS THE 13-FOOT TRAILER, DUBBED THE SERRO SCOTTY SPORTSMAN SR., OFFICIALLY PRODUCED STARTING IN 1958, THAT FINALLY PUT SERRO ON THE RIGHT TRACK.

THE 13-FOOT SPORTSMAN RETAILED AT A SHADE UNDER $600 AND QUICKLY BECAME "A BIG NAME IN LITTLE TRAILERS LIKE THE SCOTTY DOG IS A BIG NAME IN LITTLE DOGS."

THE COMPANY BOOMED IN THE 1960S AND '70S, ESTABLISHING A SCOTTY-ONLY CAMPGROUND IN 1964 NAMED SCOTTYLAND IN ROCKWOOD, PENNSYLVANIA, AND CHURNING OUT 13-, 15-, AND 18-FOOT TRAILERS FROM THREE FACTORIES IN GEORGIA, OKLAHOMA, AND PENNSYLVANIA. BY THE 1980S, THE COMPANY SHIFTED MOST OF ITS PRODUCTION TO LARGER AND BOXIER TRAILERS, ALTHOUGH A 13 1/2-FOOT MODEL WAS INTRODUCED IN 1982. TRAGEDY STRUCK IN 1997 WHEN THE REMAINING PLANT IN PENNSYLVANIA WAS LEVELED BY A FIRE. IRONICALLY, AFTER THE COMPANY (NOW KNOWN AS MOBILE CONCEPTS BY SCOTTY) WAS REBUILT, IT SHIFTED ITS PRODUCTION TO COMMERCIAL TRAILERS, THE BEST SELLING OF WHICH IS A FIRE-SAFETY HOUSE. ALTHOUGH THE WEE SCOTTYS ARE NO LONGER PRODUCED, THEY CONTINUE TO THRIVE AND SURVIVE, THANKS TO THE NATIONAL SERRO SCOTTY ORGANIZATION OF SCOTTY OWNERS, WHICH HOLDS REGULARLY SCHEDULED RALLIES AND CAMPOUTS. (MORE INFORMATION ON THE ORGANIZATION IS IN THE RESOURCE SECTION OF THIS BOOK.)

DAVID AND GOLIATH. This 1957 (first year of full production) Serro Scotty (facing, above), owned by Bob and Cindy Mott, sits next to a massive Airstream motorhome. Bob and Cindy bought the Scotty at an estate auction in 2002 for $75. **PHOTOGRAPHED AT CAMP DEARBORN, MICHIGAN.**

Luke shortened the original body by 6 inches for esthetic reasons, resulting in a living area 8 feet 6 inches long. The rear entry trailers were built in 1959 and 1960. Most Scottys were either 13 feet or 16 feet long. **PHOTOGRAPHED AT THE DEMING LOG SHOW GROUNDS, BELLINGHAM, WASHINGTON.**

THIS 12-FOOT (9-foot box) 1960 Serro Scotty Sportsman (facing, below) is one of two known surviving examples (only about a hundred were built in 1959-60). Owner Luke Hinman did a ground-up restoration, stripping the trailer down to the frame, powder-coating the frame, reframing the wood, and applying new aluminum skin.

The interior (above), which was a work in progress when photographed, is sheathed in honey-toned birch plywood. A one-burner stove provides just enough functionality for simple meals and a bit of warmth. The Scotty's original icebox was completely refinished. The holes in the cabinets are awaiting the drawers, which were being fabricated.

THIS 13-FOOT 1964 Sportsman Sr. (10-foot 6-inch-long x 6-foot-wide body) is pulled by an all-original 1955 Ford F100 with a 223-cubic-inch inline six-cylinder engine. The sea foam green is the original color. It is owned by Charles Taylor. PHOTOGRAPHED AT THE DEMING LOG SHOW GROUNDS, BELLINGHAM, WASHINGTON.

THE SCOTTY'S INTERIOR (above) is a study in simplicity. A dinette converts into an additional bed so four very friendly people can sleep comfortably, and meals are prepared on a compact two-burner stove.

AVID TROUT FISHERS Tammy and Steven Walker found this 1972 13-foot Serro Scotty Sportsman trailer in northeast Maryland. The Scotty was being used as a storage shed, but Tammy and Steven (facing) felt that is was restorable and perfect for their angling forays. They towed it to their home in Iowa, where they performed the restoration. **PHOTOGRAPHED AT CAMP DEARBORN, MICHIGAN.**

BY THE EARLY 1960S, canned hams had inevitably evolved away from their original ovoid profile toward a more space-efficient oblong shape, a trend spurred by the more angular forms already evident in automobiles of the era. Ultimately, though, for reasons of economy rather than style, the bread loaf and canned ham schools of design merged into the rather lackluster slab-sided forms that now dominate trailer design. This 1963 Fleetwing (below) is a late holdover from canned ham silhouettes of the past; its curved fore-and-aft pattern contrasts notably with the crisp lines of the Mercury Monterey built the same year. The duo is owned by Dave Mikol. PHOTOGRAPHED AT CAMP DEARBORN, MICHIGAN.

THE ANGULAR Kit Companion (facing), dating from 1966, represents the twilight of the canned ham school. By the mid-1960s, right angles ruled trailer design for both esthetic and economic reasons. Thereafter, only specialty trailers such as the Airstream and teardrop trailers would retain the curving shapes they inherited from the Streamline era. The trailer is owned by Steve Robison. PHOTOGRAPHED ON THE PLAYA OF THE BLACK ROCK DESERT NEAR GERLACH, NEVADA.

FROM THE GOLDEN AGE of travel trailers in the 1930s through the 1960s, almost all travel trailers manufactured in California were built in factories in or near sunny Los Angeles. It seems that every other building in the Los Angeles suburb of El Monte housed a trailer manufacturer. However, there were outposts of aluminum sprinkled throughout the state. A case in point was the Little Caesar Trailer Company located in sleepy Sebastopol, thirty miles north of San Francisco.

Emil and Ed Sokolis and their three brothers owned the company, which churned out a tad over 2,200 trailers from 1946 to 1955. The Little Caesar's claim to fame was its dropped axle, which resulted in a low 6-foot 10-inch profile, enabling it to slide into most garages. The company concentrated on travel trailers that were small (none longer than 14 feet) but pricy for the time. The 13-foot model illustrated in the photograph sold for $1,450 in 1951, a price just a shade less than Airstream's Cruisette. The trailer is owned by Aedan and Michael Haworth. **PHOTOGRAPHED IN ALAMEDA, CALIFORNIA.**

THE INTERIOR CONFIGURATION of the Little Caesar follows the common canned ham arrangement with a fixed double bed aft (out of view), a dinette that converts to additional sleeping accommodations, a sink, an icebox, and a Hansen three-burner propane stove. Departing from the norm, the interior surfaces are sheathed in solid honey-toned fir plywood instead of the more common 1/8-inch birch paneling that was affixed to pine ribs. The exterior aluminum was applied directly over the plywood without the use of ribs.

FOLLOWING THE Little Caesar's lead, some years later the Aristocrat Trailer Company also offered a low-slung trailer. Dubbed the Lo-Liner, the zoomy trailer was designed short enough to be housed in suburban garages and to be towed easily. This Lo-Liner's owners, Henry and Janell Diaz, are only the third owners of the trailer. The original owners from San Francisco purchased the trailer shortly after they bought a new 1963 Pontiac. After picking up the trailer from a dealer in Morgan Hill, California (about an hour south of San Francisco), they hit the road running. In the next few years, with the Lo-Liner in tow, they traveled as far as Niagara Falls and Mexico. At the end of their travels, rather than let the trailer sit and molder away, they sheltered it for twenty years in their garage before selling it in 2004.

The 10-foot-long trailer is all original. The only alterations have been a coat of polish on the exterior and the replacement of tires. The tow vehicle is a two-tone teal and abalone 1951 Pontiac Catalina beefed up with a Chevrolet 350 engine, which enables the Lo-Liner to glide effortlessly down the highway. PHOTOGRAPHED IN ALAMEDA, CALIFORNIA.

THE ALL-ORIGINAL INTERIOR is an ode to the 1960s: grooved laminated paneling, a quilted aluminum heat shield in back of the three-burner copper-tone stove sporting a copper range hood, and even a copper-rimmed kitchen light.

THE EARTHY COPPER THEME is continued with a Hadco refrigerator. The fabric covering the convertible sofa and window shades is original to the trailer, as is the carpet. Unlike many canned ham trailers of the era that are devised to shoe-horn in as many occupants as possible, the Lo-Liner is only configured to house two adults.

THE APPROPRIATELY NAMED Scotsman trailer was marketed to customers with an eye toward thriftiness. Scotsman trailers were manufactured in Gardena, California, from the early 1950s to the early 1970s. Because of the use of somewhat less-expensive materials, few have survived. Thrifty-minded couple Stuart and Kathleen Honnard purchased this 1967 14-foot model for the bargain price of $600. The compact size of the trailer has allowed the couple to take the trailer in places where larger RVs fear to tread. The tow vehicle is a 1987 Cadillac Brougham, which can tow the tidy Scotsman as if it were feather light. PHOTOGRAPHED AT THE CANYON RV PARK, ANAHEIM, CALIFORNIA.

THE INTERIOR OF THE TRAILER is a study in compact functionality. Meals are cooked on a three-burner propane stove (there is no oven–a thrifty concession) that sits atop a Dometic refrigerator (a replacement to the original icebox–another economy-minded choice). The previous owner of the Scotsman installed a small air conditioner in the front window. When it went out, Stuart and Kathleen replaced it with a newer model. Except for the wallpaper, the rest of the trailer is original.

SMALLISH CANNED-HAM-STYLE trail-
ers were sometimes built from plans featured
in handyman-oriented magazines like *Popular
Mechanics, Mechanix Illustrated,* and a host of
others. Many homebuilt models were skinned
in less-than-durable materials like plywood and
Masonite, and few have survived. Thus, this
pumpkin-colored plywood trailer built some-
time in the late 1940s or early 1950s is a rarity.
The trailer is owned by Debbie Izenman. PHOTO-
GRAPHED AT THE CANYON RV PARK, ANAHEIM,
CALIFORNIA.

DESPITE THEIR SMALL SIZE, canned ham trailers have served as temporary homes for more than a few thrifty souls. They seem to have an enduring popularity with college students on a budget. This 1,100 pound, 17-foot Tour-A-Home was manufactured in Flint, Michigan, and is owned by Don and DeAnna Anderson. DeAnna's parents purchased it new in 1958. The Tour-A-Home housed the couple when Don was attending grad school, and their daughter was born while they were living in the trailer. In 2006, Don, DeAnna, and the Tour-A-Home participated in the Historic National Road Caravan, which celebrated the two hundredth anniversary of the National Road envisioned by George Washington. They drove the entire route of the road from Maryland to Vandalia, Illinois. **PHOTOGRAPHED AT TROPICAL PALMS RESORT, KISSIMMEE, FLORIDA.**

THE INTERIOR of the Tour-A-Home on page 99 is completely original and features a propane heater, two-burner stove, icebox, sink, table, and benches. There is a three-quarter bed (out of view), and the dinette converts into an additional bed. The cabinets are made of Douglas fir plywood, and the other surfaces are sheathed in birch plywood. All of the interior decorations and utensils are from the 1950s.

IN THE 1950S, it seems that anyone who had a small shop with tools capable of doing metal and woodwork was turning out single-axle canned ham trailers. A case in point was the Sportcraft Trailer Manufacturing Company of Cortland, Ohio, which was founded by Ray Allen, who had previously manufactured trailers on the West Coast. The company rolled out small canned ham trailers between 1955 and 1960 from a factory in Orangeville, Ohio. Then they switched to larger "park" models from 1960 to 1964, which were manufactured in Clearwater, Florida. By 1965, the company had faded into the sunset. The canned ham models came in 15-, 16- , 17- , and 19-foot models. The 19-foot was the only one that was fully self-contained.

This 1957 Sportcraft 15, which sold for $995, is 6 feet 3 inches wide and has 6 feet 5 inches of headroom. The trailer sleeps five, using the typical canned ham configuration of a dinette that converts to a bed in the fore section, a full bed aft, and a child-sized hammock-like platform that hangs over the full bed. Amenities nestled into its cozy birch interior include an icebox, sink, and two-burner stove. Forrest and Jeri Bone, founders of the Tin Can Tourists, found the Sportcraft in Florida. After a bit of refurbishment, they passed the trailer to their son Terry Bone, who, along with his wife, Michelle, completed the restoration. The trailer is towed with a 1966 Ford F100 Custom Cab powered by a 302 V8 engine. PHOTOGRAPHED IN CAMP DEARBORN, MICHIGAN.

THIS TINY CORVETTE TRAILER, manufactured in El Monte, California, was photographed in America's most unusual RV community, Slab City, California. "The Slabs" is located on the grounds of an abandoned military base in Southern California's Mojave Desert. Every fall hundreds of snowbirds trickle in to enjoy the balmy weather and no-fee camping. Slab City hosts an eclectic mix of individuals and RVs, from well-heeled northerners with massive diesel-pusher motorhomes to the down-and-out with decrepit trailers and nowhere else to go. Somehow these seemingly diverse souls find a way to fit together and get along. Enterprising locals from the nearby hamlet of Niland supply the slabbers with some basic services, such as package delivery, groceries, and water. The Corvette pictured has its own water tower, appropriately labeled Rancho Not So Grande.

AT THE DAWN of the twenty-first century, Gerry and Rod Hagelund, two enterprising brothers from British Columbia, built about twenty retro-styled canned ham trailers that they dubbed the Twister. The 15-foot Twisters were modeled on the Shasta trailers manufactured in the late 1950s. The tow car of this one (above) is a 1956 Chevrolet Bel Air. **PHOTOGRAPHED IN CHICO, CALIFORNIA.**

RV-ING IS BY NO MEANS limited to Americans. Starting with the gypsies, Europeans continue to have a love affair with hitting the road in search of adventure and new horizons. Since European vehicles and roads tend to be smaller than their American counterparts, so are their travel trailers. Few are as tiny as this 1962 Knaus (facing), which is barely 7 feet long. The owners, Lowell and Janice Vivian, have dubbed the diminutive domicile the Swallow's Nest.

Despite its Lilliputian proportions, the Knaus designers have managed to wedge in a stove, sink, icebox, dinette, and sleeping for two. **PHOTOGRAPHED IN ALAMEDA, CALIFORNIA.**

THIS PAIR OF VEHICULAR GEMS is about as custom as they come. Bob Johnson, an airplane mechanic who works at a small airport in Tacoma, Washington, made the 9½-foot-long x 5-foot 11-inch-high x 6-foot-wide canned-ham-style trailer mostly from surplus and salvaged parts. Starting with a frame made from pine and fir, he applied an aluminum skin purchased from Boeing surplus. He added salvaged marine accent lights, salvaged jalousie windows, surplus aircraft running lights, and boat trailer lights. The silver gem has a birch interior and sits on modestly scaled 12-inch wheels.

Customizer Timothy Dillon of Kent, Washington, modified the automobile. His grape creation started out its life as a 1949 Lincoln with suicide doors. Tim added the fender skirts in a style sympathetic to the car's era. Then he got to work adding his own unique touches. He started by chopping down the body 4 inches and adding the side chrome tailpipes to achieve a sleek profile. One hundred fifty louvers were cut into the hood to ventilate the 454 Chevrolet engine; the original headlights were replaced with a pair extracted from a 2000 Kia Sportage; a 1954 Desoto grille was rechromed and wedged into the front; 2000 Impala door handles replaced the originals; and 1964 T-Bird seats were swapped out from the originals. The entire assemblage sits on a 1976 Camaro sub-frame resting on 17-inch whitewall tires that were custom made for the vehicle. PHOTOGRAPHED AT THE DEMING LOG SHOW GROUNDS, BELLINGHAM, WASHINGTON.

THE VINTAGE TRAILER phenomenon has become so popular that some companies are now making retro-style trailers. One of the eye-catching models is the T@B trailer manufactured by Dutchman Manufacturing, Inc., of Goshen, Indiana. Dutchman, which is a subsidiary of recreational vehicle giant Thor Industries, makes twenty different brands of trailers. Within the company, T@B stands for "Take America Back," which is somewhat ironic since the trailer is a licensed copy of the Tabbert trailer, and originator of the T@B logo, which is made in Germany. A close inspection of the T@B's accoutrements reveals a door made in Germany, a window made in Holland, and a stove made in Italy. Still, the tidy little trailer is a perfect complement to many vintage vehicles, and because of its light weight (1,600 pounds dry), it can easily be towed by today's more modestly propelled and decidedly retro-looking vehicles like the PT Cruiser, VW Bug, and Mini Cooper. The tow vehicle is a specially modified, creamy orange 1948 Ford Pickup, dubbed Peachy Keen by its owners Gordie and Terry Engelstad. PHOTOGRAPHED AT THE DEMING LOG SHOW GROUNDS, BELLINGHAM, WASHINGTON.

SHOEHORNED into the T@B's 13-foot 6-inch x 6-foot 3-inch body are a stove, refrigerator, heat pump, double bed, and dinette—all the comforts of home, except a bathroom.

GLASS
Houses

IN THE HISTORIC HOUSING WORLD, THE TERM ADAPTIVE REUSE
is often employed to describe one type of building that is converted to another, such as when an old fire station is converted to a residence. To take the process one step farther, one might use the term *adaptive recycling* to describe one thing that becomes something else, such as old tires that are ground up and mixed with asphalt, resulting in a more resilient road surface. In the RV world, there is no better example of adaptive recycling than the compact boler trailer (boler spells their name with a small "b").

The boler trailer was the brainchild of Ray Olecko of Winnipeg, Canada. Olecko had gained a measure of fame as a developer of lightweight fiberglass septic tanks as an alternative to concrete and steel ones, which were bulky and heavy, and was an avid camper and outdoorsman. While camping with his wife and two children in the late 1960s, Olecko came up with the idea of employing the same molded fiberglass technology he used to manufacture septic tanks to build a compact trailer that was big enough to shoehorn in two adults and two children. Dispensing with traditional methods of design that required complex calculations and blueprints, Olecko simply sketched out the shape on a piece of cardboard and handed the primitive drawing to his fiberglass mold maker, Sandor Dussa, with the simple command, "Make it like this." Convinced it was a good idea, Dussa and Olecko mortgaged their homes to generate start-up costs of $5,000 and set off to put their ideas into action.

Before the creation of the boler, there had been a small number of other manufacturers who had tried their hand at crafting fiberglass trailers. A company named Aalite in Benton Harbor, Michigan, created a line of one-piece fiberglass trailers as early as 1963. But none of these trailers gained a foothold, and they soon went out of business or changed their product lines.

Nevertheless, Olecko persevered. He didn't have a name for the tiny trailer, but after studying Dussa's creation, which bore a resemblance to a bowler hat, he decided to name it the boler. Changing the spelling gave the trailer a one-of-a-kind name that was easy to trademark. After adding the appropriate running gear and accessories, the tiny trailer measured a mere 13 feet long and weighed less than a thousand pounds. Olecko rolled the petite trailer in front of a number of dealers to generate orders, but the dealers were reluctant to add it to their product line since the boler's projected price of $1,400 was considerably more than the $900 for a comparably equipped aluminum trailer. Still, Olecko persisted even to the point of picking up the trailers by their hitches and dragging them around a parking lot to demonstrate their lightweight design. It paid off. Armed with a handful of orders, Olecko manufactured one hundred units that first year. The first trailers had a relatively flat roof, which makes them easy to date and identify. Olecko opted for a more arched ceiling to increase headroom, starting with the 1969 model year.

In 1969, he moved the company to a thirty-thousand-square-foot facility in Winnipeg. That year one hundred fifty units were produced, and by 1970, there were between four and five hundred bolers manufactured. In 1971, Olecko sold

BOLER

boler manufacturing franchises to two other Canadian companies in Earlton, Ontario, and Peace River, Alberta. The Winnipeg plant was churning out close to nine hundred bolers a year. By late 1971, the company had sold a U.S. franchise to Eleanor International in Wichita, Kansas. Like many inventors, Olecko yearned for new adventures and sold his share of the company to Jim Pattison, who owned Neonex Manufacturing. Neonex manufactured a number of recreational vehicles as well as mobile homes. The boler manufacturing facility was moved to a new plant in Calgary. Records are a bit sketchy, but production of trailers with the boler name ceased in 1980, after seven thousand to ten thousand units were produced.

Although there were a relatively small number of the trailers produced, thanks to their non-corroding fiberglass shell and small size, which allowed them to be stored in a protective shelter, there are still a number of the wee trailers on the road. The little trailer also has a fan club that holds two types of rallies: those exclusively for boler owners are called Boleramas; those allowing all makes of fiberglass trailers are called Glass Class Rallies.

The tiny boler was the first successful fiberglass trailer, a trailer style that continues to be manufactured to this day. Among the dozens of trailer brands that can trace their roots to the humble boler are Amerigo, Beachcomber, Bigfoot, BIOD, Burro, Casita, Cloud, Compact Jr., Companion, Eagle, Eco, Escape, Fiber Stream, Liberty, Lite House, Love Bug, MKP, Minit, Miti-Lite, Northern Lite, Oxygen, Perris Pacer, Play-Mor II, Play–Pac, Quantum, Scamp, Suntrek, Surfside, Tote 'n Tarry, Trail Mite, Trails West, Campster, Trailorboat, Trillium, U–Haul, UNIK, and Ventura.

PICTURED WITH THE 1972 BOLER is a diminutive 1958 Nash Metropolitan. The boler is owned by Rick and Janice Myer, and the Nash is owned by Mark and Rhonda Gelstein. PHOTOGRAPHED AT CAMP DEARBORN, MICHIGAN.

THIS 1978 FIBER STREAM is one of a number of similar fiberglass trailers that were manufactured in the late 1970s and continue today. Many fiberglass mold manufacturers dipped their toes into trailer manufacturing. Most trailers were a fairly modest size. Their dainty proportions, combined with the durability of fiberglass, have resulted in an amazing number of them surviving to this day. Vintage trailer enthusiasts seem to have a knack for finding them, extricating them from their moorings, and towing them home. This Fiber Stream was manufactured in Southern California in limited numbers. The company continued to manufacture trailers until 1986 or '88. Within its 16 feet are a bathroom with shower, combination gas/electric refrigerator, water heater, and three water tanks—one each for fresh, gray, and black water. True to the 1970s esthetic, the interior of the trailer is sheathed in pressboard laminate with a dark wood-grain plastic veneer and is decorated in a sunflower theme. The Fiber Stream is owned by Barbara and Donald Jussero. PHOTOGRAPHED AT THE DEMING LOG SHOW GROUNDS, BELLINGHAM, WASHINGTON.

THE 1970S were the heyday of fiberglass trailers. Seemingly dozens of manufacturers churned them out. This creation, a 1972 Compact Jr. manufactured in Chatsworth, California, has an unusual rear entry. The aft entry makes the interior configuration more like a slide-in camper than a traditional trailer. Cabinets lining both walls provide ample storage, and a dinette in the fore section converts into a double bed. The roof telescopes to provide ventilation and increased headroom. PHOTOGRAPHED AT GUAJOME COUNTY PARK, OCEANSIDE, CALIFORNIA.

DESPITE THEIR AGE DIFFERENCE, this 1937 Plymouth and 1980 boler make an attractive couple. The 17-foot boler, built by Neonex, is fully self-contained and is complete with shower, toilet, and air conditioner. The Plymouth and boler are owned by Ken Patten. PHOTOGRAPHED AT THE DEMING LOG SHOW GROUNDS, BELLINGHAM, WASHINGTON.

IN THE EARLY 1980S, rental giant U-Haul threw its hat into the fiberglass trailer ring. On January 25, 1984, U-Haul announced it was going to start renting its own brand of travel trailers made to its specifications. According to an article in the *Dayton Daily News,* the first trailers were going to be made at the rate of twelve per day by the Dayton Trailer Manufacturing Company of Dayton, Ohio. The sturdy little trailers were manufactured from 1984 to 1985 and continued to be rented by U-Haul until 1990. The trailers, which were made in 13-foot and 16-foot lengths (the 13-foot complete with toilet and sleeping for four was the most common), were durably made since U-Haul knew they would take quite a beating. U-Haul also incorporated some special features, like a swamp cooler and cabinets that could slide out to be easily cleaned.

When U-Haul decided to stop renting the tiny trailers, they painted over the U-Haul name and then offered them for sale. Thus, it's a bit hard to spot a U-Haul when motoring down the road. Restorers can usually find the painted-over labels and also the label of Rec-Vee, the company that actually handled the rentals. PHOTOGRAPHED AT THE DEMING LOG SHOW GROUNDS, BELLINGHAM, WASHINGTON.

IN 2000, while pulling a cumbersome fifth-wheel trailer on their way back from a trip, Gail Parker and her husband spied this 13-foot 1980 boler (right) in back of BrewBakers restaurant in Onaway, Michigan. The forlorn trailer seemed to speak to Gail, and she made an offer and purchased it. After the death of her husband, she sold the big fifth-wheel but held onto the boler. She travels extensively in the boler, often with her daughter and granddaughter and always with her Yorkie, Buddy. In 2001, she spent five weeks traveling all over the Maritimes and the northeastern United States. The compact size of the boler makes redecorating a frequent and fun activity. Gail reports that towing, backing up, and hooking up the boler is a breeze, and she is often the envy of owners of larger rigs. PHOTOGRAPHED AT CAMP DEARBORN, MICHIGAN.

SILVER
Gems

THE GENESIS OF THE STREAMLINED ALUMINUM TRAILER is credited to William Hawley Bowlus (1886-1967), a glider builder who was also the shop foreman at Mahoney-Ryan Aircraft, the company that built Charles Lindbergh's *Spirit of Saint Louis*. Bowlus introduced the Road Chief in 1934 and then followed it with the tiny Papoose. Both trailers were built on aircraft principles. Bowlus trailers were expensive ($750 for the diminutive Papoose to over $7,500 for the self-propelled Motor Chief) and beyond the means of most Americans. By 1936, the company was in bankruptcy. Wallace "Wally" Byam, a one-time salesman for Bowlus-Teller, purchased much of the equipment from the bankrupt company. Byam subtly reconfigured the Bowlus-Teller trailer and began marketing them under the Airstream name.

Airstream streamlined trailers were first made in 1936 and with an exception of a hiatus from production in World War II, the company has continued to manufacture trailers to the present day. Collectors were coveting the smaller vintage Airstreams, so much so that Airstream reintroduced and redesigned its line of small trailers under the Bambi name in the late 1990s.

A host of other manufacturers made large and small streamlined trailers starting immediately after World War II, but Airstream is the sole survivor. However, in the vintage trailer world, almost all streamlined trailers are extremely desirable. And contrary to almost everything else in the modern world, the smaller they are, the more they tend to cost. What follows are some stunning examples.

MOST PEOPLE ARE FAMILIAR with the distinctive shape of the Airstream trailer. These streamlined vessels always get attention whenever they are seen gliding down the road. Except for a couple of years in the early 1980s when the manufacturer decided to change the shape (the failure of the "squarestream," as it was called by its detractors, nearly put the company out of business), the trailer has retained its aerodynamic shape from the mid-1930s to the present day. The diminutive 16-foot-long Bambi demands a far higher price than its bulkier cousins, and units smaller than the Bambi, like the Cruisette and the Wee Wind, command even higher prices.

Most vintage Airstream aficionados have long believed that the smallest Airstream ever made was the Cruisette, which measured just less than 15 feet. The Cruisette was manufactured in 1951 and 1952 in Airstream's California facility and was marketed as a weekend getaway trailer. Since it had little insulation and no refrigerator or bathroom, it was little more than an aluminum tent on wheels. The no-frills package may have contributed to its less-than-stellar sales (estimates are that less than one thousand were made). Nowadays, because of its rarity, it commands a hefty price.

The Cruisette owned the crown as the tidiest Airstream until September 2004, when Airstream collector Ken Faber of Wyoming, Michigan, rolled up to the Tin Can Tourists rally in Camp Dearborn, Michigan, with a tiny silver trailer (facing) in tow. As Ken made his way to the registration area, the campground looked like a scene from the Pied Piper as dozens of rally attendees walked behind the trailer, trying to get a better look. When Ken finally parked and got out of his car, he told the audience the tale of Der Kleine Prinz, which at 13 feet is the smallest Airstream ever made.

Faber said that although the provenance of the trailer can't be absolutely verified (there are no pictures of its manufacture or an original bill-of-sale), it is clear that Airstream built the trailer in 1958 at its Jackson Center, Ohio, facility. Bob Ambrose, a retired Airstream employee, thinks the trailer was built at the request of Airstream founder Wally Byam after Byam returned from an Airstream caravan in Europe. The European connection may explain the trailer's German name "Der Kleine Prinz" (the little prince). It's unclear what happened to the tiny trailer in the 1960s, but in the 1970s, it was discovered on a used car lot and purchased for $800 by a couple from Muncie, Indiana. A few years later the couple got $1,500 in trade-in value for the Prinz towards another Airstream product, an Argosy Minuet. Thereafter, Der Kleine Prinz sat in the Berning's Trailer Sales showroom in Fort Wayne, Indiana, as an attention-getting conversation piece. Acting on a tip from a

friend, Ken Faber first saw the trailer in 1992, but it took twelve years of persistence before he finally convinced Rick Berning, the company's owner, to sell it to him.

Unique features of the trailer are the Lilliputian bathroom with shower that Airstream managed to wedge into the left rear corner, a three-burner stove, a refrigerator, a propane-fired heater, and, perhaps the most unique of all, a nameplate sporting the Der Kleine Prinz name. The nameplate is particularly noteworthy because at the time of

its manufacture in 1958, Airstream did not routinely put nameplates on its custom trailers, more evidence that it was probably Byam who commissioned the trailer.

The actual box of the trailer is 6 x 10 feet with a 6-foot 3-inch ceiling. The tidy proportions make sleeping a bit of a challenge for the 6-foot 3-inch Faber and his wife, Petey. (Ken sleeps crosswise on the floor and Petey sleeps on the bed). **PHOTO-GRAPHED IN CAMP DEARBORN, MICHIGAN.**

THESE TWO EXTRAORDINARY vehicles paired together for the photograph are an early 1935 Bowlus Road Chief owned by Gar and Mary Alice Williams and a 1935 LaSalle touring couple model 5011 (only two are known to exist) owned by Dave Mikol. The Bowlus trailer was invented by William Hawley Bowlus and manufactured by Bowlus-Teller Manufacturing Company in San Fernando, California, from 1934 to 1936. Prior to inventing the Bowlus trailer, Hawley Bowlus already had a list of achievements, including being the shop foreman at Mahoney-Ryan Airlines who supervised the construction of the *Spirit of Saint Louis.* Bowlus also constructed a number of record-breaking sailplanes.

The Bowlus-Teller line consisted of the 18-foot 6-inch Road Chief (pictured here), a 20-foot De Luxe Road Chief, an 11-foot 6-inch Papoose, a 10-foot 6-inch Trail-UR-Boat, and a motorized version of the De Luxe Road Chief, dubbed the Motor Chief. Bowlus built approximately two hundred Road Chiefs of which a couple of dozen survive. **PHOTOGRAPHED AT CAMP DEARBORN, MICHIGAN.**

RAREST OF THE RARE. This 1935 Bowlus Papoose (only four are known to exist) is a mere 11 feet 6 inches in length, 6 feet wide, and 7 feet high. It weighs in at seven hundred pounds. Like the Road Chief, the Papoose is entered from the fore end. The present owners found it in abysmal condition—it had been painted and had numerous dents and pits—but through hours of toil, they restored it to pristine condition. The Papoose is owned by Leo and Marlys Keoshian and is towed with a 1934 Packard Coupe Roadster. **PHOTOGRAPHED ON THE STANFORD UNIVERSITY CAMPUS, PALO ALTO, CALIFORNIA.**

Every square inch is utilized in the Papoose interior. There is a small galley at the entrance (out of view), and the dinette converts into a bed. Four windows, two of which serve as skylights, provide ample illumination. The warm wood paneling gives the Papoose the feel of a very cozy summer cabin. The owners have decorated the trailer with period accessories, including a portrait of New Deal president Franklin D. Roosevelt, 1930s tableware, and the owners' most treasured trailer accessory: a cookbook for trailerites titled *Meals on Wheels*.

IN 1948, Wally Byam was ready to surge forward with Airstream once again as Airstream Trailers Incorporated, which he opened in a small factory near the Metropolitan Airport in Van Nuys, a suburb of Los Angeles. His first product was the Airstream Liner, which was essentially the same trailer as the Curtis Wright Clipper and the Silver Streak Clipper. While other trailer manufacturers were looking at building big, bigger, and biggest trailers, Byam saw sales potential for a smaller trailer that was suited for weekend camping rather than extended stays. The result was the Wee Wind, which used a lengthwise spine of tubular steel (seen protruding from beneath the rib rail on the aft end) to support the floor members and ribs. After problems developed with torsional flexing, later units adopted a more conventional ladder-type frame. Airstream marketed a series of "Wind" models during the late '40s and into the '50s, including the Westwind, Southwind, Whirlwind, and Tradewind. At 16 feet, the Wee Wind was the smallest, and, thanks to its tubular frame, it was also the lightest (1,200 pounds) Airstream ever made. The 1948 Airstream Wee Wind is towed by a 1955 GMC Pickup with a 350-cubic-inch engine 700 Ford D transmission. The pair is owned by Ken and Petey Faber. PHOTOGRAPHED AT CAMP DEARBORN, MICHIGAN.

ALTHOUGH TEARDROP and canned ham trailers are often built by do-it-yourselfers, streamlined aluminum trailers with their complex curves and riveted construction are almost always built in formal shops and factories that have experience with aircraft construction techniques. Thus, this one-of-a-kind tiny streamlined trailer is a rarity and one of the gems in Vince Martinico's Auburn Trailer Collection. Martinico found the 12½-foot trailer, built in 1936 ("made in 1936" was painted on the rear panel), near Walla Walla, Washington. Martinico stripped the paint, polished the aluminum, and replaced the windows (which pulled up with a strap) with crank windows from a 1932 Ford. Otherwise the trailer's exterior is all original. Martinico restored the birch-paneled interior, added Mercedes green-leather cushions and installed marnoleum (a linoleum product that would have been used in the 1930s), and replaced many of the weathered metal parts with engine-turned copper (a swirled polishing technique). **PHOTOGRAPHED IN SACRAMENTO, CALIFORNIA.**

AT 16½ FEET and weighing 2,500 pounds, the Pacer was the most diminutive trailer that Airstream manufactured in 1958, 1959, and 1960. In 1961, the Pacer was replaced by the Bambi. All of these modestly scaled trailers are highly desirable among collectors, and finder's fees are often given to silver sleuths who discover them. The trailer, dubbed "Polly Pacer," is owned by Linda and Don Coolich. PHOTOGRAPHED AT CAMP DEARBORN, MICHIGAN.

OF ALL THE commonly available Airstreams, none is as desirable as the Bambi. Its diminutive size (16 feet) makes it a breeze to tow, and it has all of the necessities (albeit in modest scale) for comfortable camping. Indeed, it is the smallest Airstream to sport a fully equipped bathroom. This 1961 Bambi (facing), according to its owner, has the earliest-known Bambi serial number. There were less than eight hundred Bambis manufactured between 1961 and 1963. In 1964, Airstream added another 12 inches to the Bambi and rechristened it the Bambi II. The Bambi owned by Patrick and Joanne Ewing has a dry weight of less than two thousand pounds, thus the Ewings' 1930 four-cylinder Model A Ford is quite capable of towing it.

PHOTOGRAPHED AT THE DEMING LOG SHOW GROUNDS, BELLINGHAM, WASHINGTON.

THE YEAR 1963 was the last year of the 16-foot Bambi, after which it evolved into the 17-foot Bambi II. The owners of this 1963 Bambi (above) bought it from a New Holland, Michigan, man in 1989, who had purchased it from an Elkhart, Indiana, Airstream dealer that was going out of business. In the last few years, this Bambi has won a number of awards at trailer shows and has been one of the featured stars at automobile shows. The owners consider it their most treasured possession. The Bambi is owned by Ken and Petey Faber. PHOTOGRAPHED AT CAMP DEARBORN, MICHIGAN.

THE INTERIOR of the 16-foot Bambi is actually only 13 feet long, since trailers are commonly measured from the hitch to the bumper. At the rear of the trailer (above) is a combination stove and refrigerator. To the right of the stove is a fully functional bathroom complete with shower, configured much like the bathroom on a small boat. The Bambi will, surprisingly, sleep four: the sofa on the right folds down to a double bed and the dinette (out of view, behind) converts into another double bed. Petey Faber, one of the Bambi's owners, is an apt watercolorist and spends much of her time at vintage trailer rallies, sketching other participants' trailers.

BAMBIS ARE PARTICULARLY popular with classic car collectors. Their gentle curves blend well with the automobile styles of the late 1940s through the mid-1950s. This 1963 Bambi (facing) is towed by a perfectly suited 1947 Mercury woody station wagon owned by Michael and Aedan Haworth. PHOTOGRAPHED AT THE SILVER SOCIAL, CALISTOGA, CALIFORNIA.

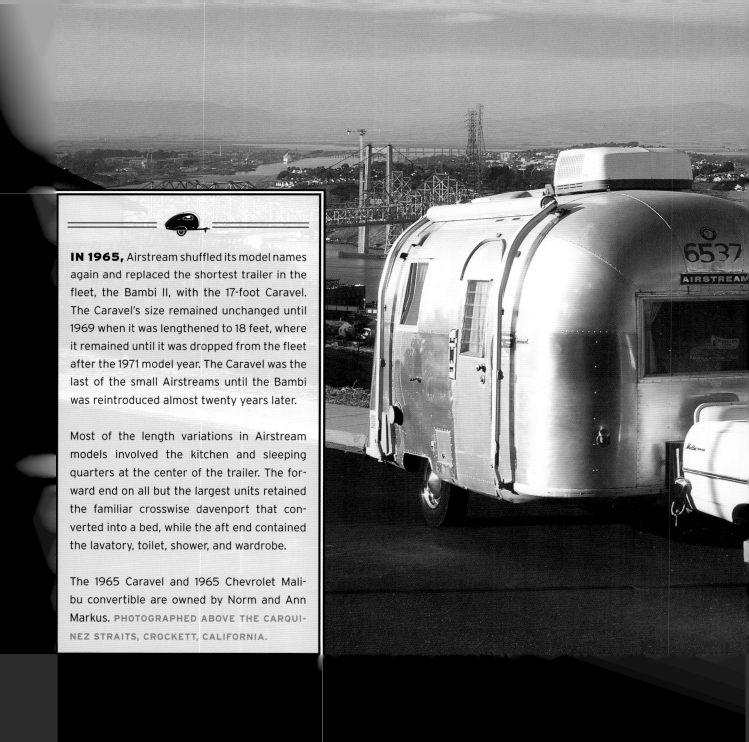

IN 1965, Airstream shuffled its model names again and replaced the shortest trailer in the fleet, the Bambi II, with the 17-foot Caravel. The Caravel's size remained unchanged until 1969 when it was lengthened to 18 feet, where it remained until it was dropped from the fleet after the 1971 model year. The Caravel was the last of the small Airstreams until the Bambi was reintroduced almost twenty years later.

Most of the length variations in Airstream models involved the kitchen and sleeping quarters at the center of the trailer. The forward end on all but the largest units retained the familiar crosswise davenport that converted into a bed, while the aft end contained the lavatory, toilet, shower, and wardrobe.

The 1965 Caravel and 1965 Chevrolet Malibu convertible are owned by Norm and Ann Markus. PHOTOGRAPHED ABOVE THE CARQUINEZ STRAITS, CROCKETT, CALIFORNIA.

THIS STYLISH DUO is a 1935 Auburn Boattail Speedster replicar with hotrod Lincoln running gear and a rare 1950 18-foot Silver Streak Clipper trailer. Owner James Hamilton spied the trailer on the Navajo Indian Reservation near Chinle, Arizona, and left a note on it offering to buy it. The owner didn't contact him, so he journeyed back to Arizona a year later, tracked down the owner, plunked down $500, and brought it home to Seattle. He worked on the restoration for about a year. He gutted the entire interior but found that the exterior was reasonably intact, requiring only minor repairs and a good polishing.

The Silver Streak trailer company, headquartered in El Monte, California, operated from 1949 until 1997. It was started by three investors who bought the Curtis Wright Industries trailer company (no relation to Curtiss-Wright Aircraft Corporation). Silver Streak was a boutique trailer company, never making more than a few hundred trailers a year. Most of the trailers were in the 20-foot-plus category, which makes this 18-foot model dating from 1950 a rare bird. PHOTOGRAPHED AT THE DEMING LOG SHOW GROUNDS, BELLINGHAM, WASHINGTON.

THE BAMBI MAY BE the most sought-after vintage Airstream, but it seems that the Globe Trotter has been the most adaptable Airstream. This 1965 Globe Trotter's 19-foot length makes it reasonably easy to tow and navigate and also provides ample interior space to move around in and to tailor to the owner's tastes. The trailer is owned by Tom and Mary Bamborough. PHOTO-GRAPHED AT CAMP DEARBORN, MICHIGAN.

DESPITE SQUARISH LINES, the twenty-first-century Airstream trailer—a 2006 Bambi Quicksilver edition is pictured here—still bears a clear family resemblance to its prewar ancestors. Unlike many industrial creeds, Wally Byam's policy of evolutionary refinement has somehow survived both fluctuating economies and newfangled managerial theories. Today, Airstream has become an icon of America, much like Coca-Cola or Levi's. Indeed, Airstream has become as synonymous with a shiny trailer as Scotch has with adhesive tape or Kleenex has with facial tissue. Byam's worldview was also ahead of its time; he saw travel not merely as a pleasurable pastime but as a means to further understanding among diverse people. In 1960, two years before his death, Byam declared, "Whether we like it or not, any fool can see that this earth is gradually becoming one world. Nobody knows what the form of the 'one' will be, but it's going to be one or none." The events of the early twenty-first century have certainly proved him right. The Airstream and tow vehicle (a 1999 Chevrolet Blazer) are owned by Mardy Ireland. PHOTOGRAPHED IN ALAMEDA, CALIFORNIA.

OVER THERE

and Elsewhere

NORTH AMERICANS AREN'T THE ONLY ONES POSSESSED WITH THE

vagabond spirit. Centuries before macadam was invented, gypsies roamed the

deeply rutted roads of the European countryside. That oft-maligned group got

its name from a geographic error: most folks thought they originally came from

Egypt (hence the "gyp" in "gypsy") when in fact they came from India. Nowadays,

vintage gypsy wagons, know as gypsy caravans in the United Kingdom and

roulottes in France, command steep prices and the supply exceeds the demand.

Enterprising individuals are now making new gypsy wagons in the old style.

Throughout Europe, citizens looking for an escape from the cities crowd the highways on weekends and holidays with their caravans (trailers) and campervans (motorhomes). The meticulous Germans manufacture a number of superbly designed compact caravans that tow easily behind almost any vehicle. The high-speed autobahns allow them to quickly motor to almost any destination.

Across the channel in England and Scotland, there are numerous caravan clubs, micro-caravan clubs, and, in recent years, vintage caravan clubs. Some Brits claim that they are the birthplace of caravans, citing the Eccles caravan

(the company still exists today), fifty units of which were produced in Birmingham, England, in 1919.

The Brits may lay claim to the first caravans, but it's the Aussies who have the most room to roam. With almost three million square miles of countryside for its 31 million residents to wander in (the contiguous United States has slightly over three million square miles for its 300 million residents) and few formal lodging options away from the larger cities, a caravan or camper is almost a necessity for Aussies who want to venture into the outback.

THIS ERIBA PUCK (facing) manufactured in Bad Waldsee, Germany, is a product of the Hymer Group, which manufactures a number of caravans and campers. The Eriba line of compact caravans dates from 1956 and continues to this day. The 10 x 5-foot Puck has a lightweight fiberglass shell and can be pulled with almost any vehicle. The early models of the caravan had a dry weight of about five hundred pounds. The Puck sleeps two and is equipped with an icebox, stove, sink, and storage cabinets. The Puck is towed by a vintage Citroën 2CV.

LIKE MANY OF THE TEAR-DROPS, the Berkeley Caravette had a very brief tenure. Only about two hundred units of the all-metal caravan were made. The Caravette, manufactured from 1952 to 1954, was the brainchild of Charles Panter, a designer at Berkeley Coachworks in Biggleswade, Bedfordshire, England. Panter devised a system of interchangeable bodies, all of which could fit on the same frame. The customer had a choice of a teardrop body, a boat transporter, or a simple hauling trailer. Panter's interchangeable body system apparently didn't perform as well as advertised and, combined with a public that wasn't ready to embrace the tiny trailers, the Caravette exited the scene as quickly as it arrived. In recent years, thanks to the revival of vintage caravans, the Caravette has become highly desirable among collectors. This Caravette is towed with a Citroën 2CV, a model manufactured by French automaker Citroën from 1948 until 1990. The stylish duo (above) is owned by Steve Pepper. PHOTOGRAPHED IN NORTH YORKSHIRE, ENGLAND.

March 12, 1953 MOTOR CYCLING

With eight holding down bolts removed the "Caravette" can be lifted from its chassis.

A canvas extension, erected in a few minutes provides additional living or sleeping accommodation.

Offering far less wind resistance than a normal caravan, the "Caravette" is of the right dimensions for motorcycle touring, and weighs less than 5 cwt.

A THREE-WHEEL BOND pulls a Falcon Sleeper (above). Not a true teardrop (there is no galley), the Sleeper is, as advertised, strictly for sleeping. Its 4 x 6-foot body is just large enough for a mattress (available as an add-on). The Sleeper, which weighs about two hundred fifty pounds, is available as a kit for about $2,000 or can be purchased assembled for an additional $400. The Sleeper is towed by a three-wheeled Bond 4-Seater Saloon, manufactured by Bond Cars Ltd., Preston, Lancashire, England.

FACING:

A FALCON SLEEPER (upper left) is towed by an Isetta. Renzo Rivolta developed Isettas during 1952–53 in Milan, Italy. Rivolta manufactured refrigerators under the ISO name and thus named his vehicular creation Isetta ("little ISO"). BMW took over production in 1955, and eventually other factories were opened in the UK and Brazil. Production of the thrifty three-wheeled vehicle ceased in 1962.

A HONDA 600 (upper right) dating from the early 1970s tows this Falcon Sleeper. Although the Honda has a modest 45 horsepower, it's more than enough to pull the two-hundred-fifty-pound sleeper.

THIS COMPACT 8 x 5-foot Fisher Holivan (lower left) was manufactured in the UK. The Holivan is easily identifiable by its quilted center panel.

A THREE-WHEELED RELIANT Robin (lower right) dating from the 1970s tows a trailer of a similar style. The trailer was no doubt custom made by the owner to be sympathetic to the Reliant's styling.

A TRABANT CAR (facing, above) made in East Germany (Trabant translates to "servant" or "companion") tows a Predom caravan. The homely but loveable Trabants were manufactured from the mid-1950s until 1991. Predom caravans are manufactured by Freedom Caravans, Queensville, Staffordshire, England.

DESPITE FREQUENTLY GLOOMY conditions (facing, below) (the Highlands experience measurable rainfall two hundred and fifty days a year), the Scottish people are avid RVers and many accommodations are open year-round. Caravans and campervans often fill the caravan parks to bursting during summer months and on weekends. **PHOTOGRAPHED AT BRAIDHAUGH CARAVAN PARK, CRIEFF, SCOTLAND.**

THE BUNGALOW TOURIST PARK (above) near Ulladulla, New South Wales, Australia, caters to a variety of travelers, from those who prefer a bolted-down cabin, to those who want to move their caravan in for a few nights, to those who have a semipermanent mooring for their caravan.

THIS GYPSY CARAVAN (known as a roulotte in France) is nestled under a protective cover at the Mas dou Pastre Bed and Breakfast in the south of France. Wedged into the compacted living quarters are a double bed and even a bathroom (out of view). The roulotte dates from 1900.

THE ROULOTTE below was restored in 2000 by Jeanne Bayol, who found it at a fairground. It is now permanently moored at the Mas dou Pastre Bed and Breakfast.

The kitchen of the roulotte was removed and replaced with a bathroom.

Most of the furniture and accessories of the roulotte's sleeping quarters were intact when found by Bayol. After a full restoration of the surfaces, Bayol added an assortment of fabrics and accessories sympathetic to the gypsy style.

A tidy alcove marks its entry. Despite its Lilliputian proportions, a tiny sink has been wedged in. Bold, cheerful colors and a profusion of accessories are true to the gypsy spirit.

JEANNE BAYOL created this custom-made open-air roulotte. In addition to restoring gypsy wagons, Bayol also builds them from the ground up. They are for sale either as completely accessorized wagons or as basic wagons that await the owner's individual touch. Most of Bayol's creations are fully enclosed.

THREE VINTAGE GYPSY CARAVANS (above), one found and restored by the owners and two restored by Jeanne Bayol, have been turned into a unique addition to the Mas dou Pastre Bed and Breakfast in the south of France. (For more information on the Mas dou Pastre, check the Resource section at the end of this book.)

THE HORSE-DRAWN GYPSY WAGONS may be no more, but thanks to James Nelson, folks can have a modern-day version (facing, above left). By trade, James is a sign painter and, according to his business card, moonlights as a brain surgeon and builder of gypsy caravans. James has created more than a dozen gypsy wagons; some are mounted on conventional vans and some are stand-alone trailers. All of them are true to the gypsy spirit and have real stained-glass windows, rich wood interiors, and whimsical detailing. The tow vehicle in this photograph is a 2002 twelve-passenger, one-ton

Dodge van. After tearing off the roof, James constructed the shell of mahogany and pine so that it was high enough to stand in but not high enough to cause instability.

The gypsy trailer, perfect for an itinerant fortune-teller, measures 7 x 10 feet and is constructed of mahogany and pine atop a steel frame. The same grooved plywood used in the van is used throughout the trailer's interior to simulate wainscoting. While the crystal ball, metallic fabrics, crystals, and candles do not come with the trailer, they are readily available at any well-stocked gypsy emporium. **PHOTOGRAPHED AT THE FLYWHEELERS PARK, AVON PARK, FLORIDA.**

THE ENTRANCES of all roulottes (facing, above right) dating from the nineteenth century have two indispensable accessories, a colored glass lantern and a good luck charm bell.

JAMES NELSON'S 2007 gypsy trailer creation follows the form of trailers he made in previous years, but it has its own one-of-a-kind accoutrements and accessories. Highlights of the 2007 model include the usual assortments of baubles and beads plus redwood trim, custom-made real stained-glass windows, and oriental rugs from Iraq acquired by way of a yard sale. All of Nelson's trailers are built on a custom 12 x 7-foot frame and are equipped with a torsion bar suspension, electric brakes, and his own signature gypsy door. **PHOTOGRAPHED AT CAMP DEARBORN, MICHIGAN.**

Resources

Classic and Vintage Trailers

BOLER TRAILERS
www.geocities.com/bolerama

FIBERGLASS TRAILERS
www.fiberglassrv.com

GYPSY TRAILERS
United States resource:
www.gypsytrailers.com

French resource:
www.jeanne-bayol.com

Bed and breakfast with gypsy trailer:
www.masdupastre.com

SERRO SCOTTY TRAILERS
www.nationalserroscotty.org

SHASTA TRAILERS
www.vintageshastas.com

TEARDROPS
www.adventureteardrops.com
www.azteardrops.com
www.cozycruiser.com
www.cucampers.com
www.desertteardrops.com
www.golittleguy.ca
www.happytrailers.com
www.northernteardroptrailers.com

www.redtrailers.com
www.retroteardrops.com
www.rollinoak.com
www.snuzbox.com
www.socalteardrops.com
www.tab-rv.com
www.teardropparts.com
www.teardroptrailers.net
www.teardrops.net
www.wee-kender.com

Vintage Airstream

AIRSTREAM TRAILERS
www.airstreamtrailers.com

PHOTO ARCHIVES AND MODEL INDEX
www.vintageairstream.com

VINTAGE AIRSTREAM
www.vintageairstream.com

VINTAGE AIRSTREAMER
www.vintageairstreamer.com

Media in the United States and Canada

AIRSTREAM LIFE
www.airstreamlife.com

CAMPING LIFE
www.campinglife.com

ESCAPEES MAGAZINE
www.escapees.com/magazine.asp

GYPSY JOURNAL
www.gypsyjournal.net

HIGHWAYS MAGAZINE
www.goodsamclub.com

OUT WEST NEWSPAPER
www.outwestnewspaper.com

RV JOURNAL
www.rvjournal.com

RV LIFE
www.rvlife.com

RV TIMES
www.rvtimes.com

RVTV
www.rvtv.ca

TRAILER LIFE
www.trailerlife.com

WORKAMPER NEWS
www.workamper.com

Dealers, Suppliers, and Repairs

ARIZONA RV SALVAGE
www.azrvinc.com

CAMPING WORLD
www.campingworld.com

DAYTON TAYLOR
www.vintagetrailercrazy.com

DOMETIC (RV APPLIANCES)
www.dometic.com

DOUG'S VINTAGE TRAILERS
www.dougsvintagetrailers.com

FUNKY JUNK FARMS
(Vintage RV Rental)
www.funkyjunkfarms.com

**GYPSY CARAVAN
BED AND BREAKFAST**
www.masdupastre.com

GYPSY CARAVAN SALES (FRANCE)
www.jeanne-bayol.com

MEL TRAILER
www.meltrailer.com

RV COLLISION CENTER
www.rvcollisioncenter.com

TIMELESS TRAVEL TRAILER
www.timelesstraveltrailers.com

TRAILERWORKS
www.trailerworks.biz

VINCE MARTINICO
(Vintage RV Collection;
Rentals and Sales)
www.auburntrailercollection.org

VINTAGECAMPERS
www.vintagecampers.com

VINTAGE TRAILER SUPPLY
www.vintagetrailersupply.com

VINTAGE VACATIONS
www.vintage-vacations.com

Clubs and Organizations

FUN ROADS
(Exhaustive List of Clubs,
Organizations, and Owners)
www.funroads.com/club/viewClub.jhtml

SISTERS ON THE FLY
www.sistersonthefly.com

TIN CAN TOURISTS ORGANIZATION
www.tincantourists.com

VINTAGE AIRSTREAM CLUB
www.airstream.net

Museums

NATIONAL AUTOMOBILE MUSEUM
www.automuseum.org

NETHERCUTT MUSEUM
www.nethercuttcollection.org

PETERSEN AUTOMOTIVE MUSEUM
www.petersen.org

PIONEER VILLAGE
www.pioneervillage.org

RV/MH HERITAGE FOUNDATION, INC.
www.rv-mh-hall-of-fame.org